PRECIOUS ARE HIS SHEEP

by Lea Fowler

IBSN: 0-89137-463-9

DEDICATED TO:

The Good Shepherd

Gratitude

To my daughter, Becky, my co-author, my fellow-laborer, my secretary, and one of my best friends.

To Connie for her help in editing.

To Bennie Whitehead and the Quality Publishing Company for giving an unknown author in the Maine woods a chance!

To Earlene, my dear friend, who is going through the "valley of the shadow of death," fearing no evil.

To my dear family, Russ, Tom, Judy, Becky, and all those wonderful grandchildren and great grandchildren.

To all my dear sisters out there—this is for you.

TABLE OF CONTENTS

Prologue

As I grow older, I find myself so comforted to know that Jesus, our Shepherd, looks at us as sheep. He sees our vulnerabilities, our defenseless natures, our dangers of wandering off the precipices of life.

We start out as lambs. "Like a shepherd, He will tend His flock, in his arms He will gather the lambs, and carry them in His bosom; He will gently lead the nursing ewes" (Isaiah 40:11).

God looks on all of His children as lambs, for He says, "Go your way; behold, I send you out as lambs in the midst of wolves" (Luke 10:3).

Though we often displease and even anger our Lord, His everlasting love and kindness surround the sheep-fold. "In an outburst of anger I hid My face from you for a moment; but with everlasting loving kindness I will have compassion on you," says the Lord, your Redeemer (Isaiah 54:8).

The Lord is our Shepherd!

Prologue

CHAPTER 1

THE GENTLENESS OF THE LAMB OF GOD

Prophecy was foretold of what sort of a man Jesus, the Shepherd, would be.

> *Surely our griefs He Himself bore,*
> *And our sorrows He carried;*
> *Yet we ourselves esteemed Him stricken,*
> *Smitten of God, and afflicted.*
> *But He was pierced through for our transgressions,*
> *He was crushed for our iniquities;*
> *The chastening for our well-being fell upon Him,*
> *And by His scourging we are healed.*
> *All of us like sheep have gone astray,*
> *Each of us has turned to his own way;*
> *But the Lord has caused the iniquity of us all*
> *To fall on Him.*
> *He was oppressed and He was afflicted,*
> *Yet He did not open His mouth;*
> *Like a lamb that is led to slaughter,*
> *And like a sheep that is silent before its shearers,*
> *So He did not open His mouth (Isaiah 53:4-7).*

We see that prophecy fulfilled on the day of His death as Herod questioned Him. "And He questioned Him at some length; but He answered Him nothing" (Luke 23:9).

"And Pilate was questioning Him again, saying, 'Do you make no answer? See how many charges they bring against you!' But Jesus made no further answer, so that Pilate was astonished" (Mark 15:4-5).

"And while He was being accused by the chief priests and elders, He made no answer. Then Pilate said to Him, 'Do you not hear how many things they testify against you?' And He did not answer him with regard to even a single charge, so that the governor was quite amazed" (Matthew 27:12-14).

WHY DOES JESUS CALL CHRISTIANS SHEEP?

Sheep are not fighters but are followers. They are not clever; they are not destructive. Rather, they are just helpless. They are not able to defend themselves or care for themselves—nor are we.

If a sheep gets its head caught in a fence, it will push forward but not back up and extract its head. If a shepherd raises up one leg for one sheep to jump over and then puts his leg back down, many sheep will jump at the same spot, although the shepherd has lowered his leg. They blindly follow, and so do we.

SHEEP ARE VULNERABLE

Do we really know how vulnerable we are? Here today, gone tomorrow. Our lives are like a puff of smoke. Three score and ten years are counted a long life—seventy years. Medical science, through God's wisdom, has taught us how to live a little longer than man used to live.

> *"Lord, make me to know my end,*
> *and what is the extent of my days,*
> *let me know how transient I am.*
> *Behold, thou hast made my days as handbreadths,*
> *and my lifetime as nothing in Thy sight.*
> *Surely every man at his best is a mere breath.*
> *Surely every man walks about as a phantom;*
> *Surely they make an uproar for nothing;*
> *He amasses riches, and does not know who will gather them" (Psalm 39:4-6).*

Sheep cannot fight; they cannot defend themselves. When they are scared, they just panic and run. They must have daily care and constant protection or they will die.

I have heard it said that if a sheep gets turned over and cannot roll back to its feet, its digestive juices cause a quick death. (Could this be why the shepherd left the 99 and searched for the lost sheep?)

ENEMIES

The harmless sheep have many enemies. Predators follow the flock continually. (We read of David, the shepherd boy, slaying the lion and the bear in his protection of his father's flock.) God often likens men to wolves in sheep's clothing, who wish to destroy the flock. "Beware of the false prophets who come to you in sheep's clothing but inwardly are ravenous wolves. You will know them by their fruits" (Matthew 7:15,16a).

SHREWD SHEEP

"Behold, I send you out as sheep in the midst of wolves, therefore be shrewd as serpents, and innocent as doves" (Matthew 10:16). This seems to be a curious adjective for a sheep—shrewd. To be shrewd is to be prudent, careful, aware of danger. How can we be called shrewd sheep? By always having our eyes on the Shepherd. By being assured that the straight and narrow path, though often difficult, is the only safe way—the only safe way home. "Therefore be careful how you walk not as unwise men, but as wise" (Ephesians 5:15). The TEV says it this way, "So pay close attention to how you live. Don't live like ignorant men, but like wise men." The Jerusalem Bible says, "So be very careful about the sort of lives you lead, like intelligent and not like senseless people. This may be a wicked age, but your lives should redeem it."

We should ever be aware that we shall reap whatever we sow, that "God keeps a 'writin' all the time" and that God is not mocked (fooled). His light is always shining to lead us, but we will get lost in the dark if we are not shrewd.

In conclusion, aren't we glad that God thinks of us as sheep? That He carries a rod, not to beat us, but to rescue us from danger? That He promises to feed us, clothe us, and protect us from the predators? I know this is a constant comfort to me.

I'm too old to be a lamb—
Too old to fit that category.
But I'm never too old to be a sheep
And spend eternity in glory.
Lea Fowler

Read or sing together:

BRING THEM IN

Hark! 'tis the Shepherd's voice I hear,
Out in the desert dark and drear,
Calling the lambs who've gone astray,
Far from the Shepherd's fold away.

Who'll go and help this Shepherd kind,
Help Him the little lambs to find?
Who'll bring the lost ones to the fold,
Where they'll be sheltered from the cold?

Out in the desert hear their cry,
Out on the mountain wild and high;
Hark! 'tis the Master speaks to thee:
"Go find my lambs where'er they be."

Chorus:

Bring them in, Bring them in, Bring them in from the fields of sin!
Bring them in, Bring them in, Bring the little ones to Jesus.

QUESTIONS FOR DISCUSSION

1. Are sheep easily fooled?

2. What is the only way for sheep to guarantee their safety?

3. How does God defend His people, His sheep?

CHAPTER 2

THE FLOCK

"And all the nations will be gathered before Him and He will separate them from one another, as the shepherd separates the sheep from the goats; and He will put the sheep on His right, and the goats on the left. Then the King will say to those on His right, 'Come, you who are blessed of My Father, inherit the kingdom prepared for you from the foundation of the world' " (Matthew 25:32-34).

Aren't all Christians His sheep? We want to be. Often we die, thinking we are safe when we are not. "Not every one who says to me, 'Lord, Lord,' will enter the kingdom of heaven, but he who does the will of My Father who is in heaven' " (Matthew 7:21).

WHAT GOATS AND SHEEP HAVE IN COMMON

They were both used for animal sacrifices under the old law. They resemble each other. They are mountainous creatures, both feeding from pastures.

They supply physical good for mankind. Their hair or wool is useful. Their milk is necessary. Their flesh is desirable for both meat and leather goods. Most of us have tasted mutton and goat meat.

They are both often shepherded and are still found in the Middle East. They are cud-chewing animals, and both were numbered with the clean animals, fit for man's food by God and for sacrifices.

THEIR DIFFERENCES

They are separated at night. The goat does not answer the shepherd's voice. Goats also do not mate with sheep. "The wild goats are more sure-footed and adventurous. They tend to get into impossible places. They feed not only on herbs but shrubs and small trees. They stand erect as they eat the tree leaves. They are more destructive and are largely responsible for the deforested condition of Judea and Lebanon."

"One of the older, wild goats is the leader of the flock. When he tires, he is replaced for awhile" (The International Standard Bible Encyclopedia).

DEMON GOATS

Demons were likened to goats in Leviticus 17:7. "And they shall no longer sacrifice their sacrifices to the goat demons with which they play the harlot. This shall be a permanent statute to them throughout their generations."

Matthew Henry, one of my favorite Bible commentators, says that the children of Israel had learned in Egypt to revere the goat demons. "The word, demon, signifies rough and hairy goats, because it is probable that in that shape the evil spirits often appeared to them, to invite their sacrifices to the demons and to signify their acceptance of them."

Satan has many disguises. In Genesis we see him in the form of a snake, tempting Eve. He also deceives with his appearance as an angel of light. "And no wonder, for even Satan disguises himself as an angel of light" (2 Corinthians 11:14).

Although goats are separated from the sheep at night, they do travel with them during the day. The flock follows the shepherd as he chooses the pastures and watering holes.

But, the wild goats choose their own leader, run into difficult places and are very destructive.

So, we don't want to be a goat that walks with the flock in the light but is separated by the dark—clean and yet eventually unclean. Walking with the sheep—but never a sheep. Walking with the sheep—but really a goat.

Many people, the majority of people, could be compared to the wild goats, who choose their own leader, their own destructive way, and eventually wind up sitting among the ruins of their own making.

THE POOR

He started His life in the flesh in a stable. There was no room for Him in the inn. How sad to picture the innkeeper turning away a young husband with a pregnant wife!

There is STILL room for Him *in the stables.* "Listen, my beloved brethren, did not God choose the poor of this world to be rich in faith and heirs of the kingdom which He promised to those who love Him? But you have dishonored the poor man. . .but if you show partiality, you are committing sins and are convicted by the law as transgressors" (James 2:5-6).

Jesus taught us that we will always have the poor with us. In this day and age of beautiful homes, good jobs, and money in the bank, we are seeing an ever increasing number of the homeless. Welfare helps—but not enough!

Few rich, or wise, are even called to follow Him. "For consider your calling, brethren, that there were not many wise according to the flesh, not many mighty, not many noble; but God has chosen the foolish things of the world to shame the wise, and God has chosen the weak things of the world to shame the things which are strong" (1 Corinthians 1:26-27).

But, our Shepherd, who could confound the wisdom of the doctors, though He was only 12 years old, chose the simple way and the simple people to follow Him. It has always been that the "wise of the world," those intellectually elite—always in pursuit of knowledge, are simply not drawn to the simplicity of God's Word. And how heartbreaking it also is when some of the sons of our finest preachers become lost in this same pursuit of worldly wisdom. Oh, how many parents' hearts have been broken!

> *It is these things that we talk about, not using the expressions of the human intellect but those which the Holy Spirit teaches us, explaining spiritual things to those who are spiritual.*
>
> *But the unspiritual man simply cannot accept the matters which the Spirit deals with—they just don't make sense to him, for, after all, you must be spiritual to see spiritual things (1 Corinthians 2:13-14) (Phillips).*

He had no place to lay His head when He began His ministry, nor did the apostles. Peter once said, "Silver and gold have I none." Judas carried their little money bag and dipped his hand daily in the till. (What did it profit him? Suicide.)

HIS DAILY LIFE

Jesus came to serve, not to be served. He left us the example of service in every phase of our lives. *Your* great reward will be on the other side. Your blessings and your crown will come when He comes back.

We are by nature—takers. Watch a baby. He yells when he wants service, and nothing will satisfy him until he receives what he is yelling for.

We often enter the kingdom still seeking pearls, but often not the figurative "pearls of wisdom." We are competitive in the pursuit of *things*—not for stars in a crown. Jesus loves to give us the desires of our heart (Psalm 37:4). However, we must not be so wrapped up in the things of the world that will all someday burn.

CALL NO MAN MASTER

Jesus speaks about the scribes (lawyers) and Pharisees who have "seated themselves in the chair of Moses." In other words, they sat down to govern. They were often merciless; they were show offs; they sought the name, "Rabbi."

But, Jesus said that only One is our teacher and that we are all brethren. In Matthew 23:8, He says, "But do not be called Rabbi; for One is your Teacher, and you are all brethren. . .and do not be called leaders; for One is your Leader, that is, Christ."

Just a brother, never a scholar, never a doctor of religion, but ever a student. "But the greatest among you shall be your servant, and whoever exalts himself shall be humbled; and whoever humbles himself shall be exalted" (Matthew 23:11,12).

The most knowledgeable person in the Scriptures still knows very little. When we study, we are delving into the mind of God, and the Spirit helps us to understand what our limited minds can grasp. "For as the heavens are higher than the earth, so are My ways higher than your ways, and My thoughts than your thoughts" (Isaiah 55:9).

"If anyone supposes that he knows anything, he has not yet known as he ought to know; but if anyone loves God, he is known by Him" (1 Corinthians 8:2,3). Isn't that comforting?

So, we are brothers, hopefully students, gaining knowledge and understanding as we realize how little we know. I love this scripture: "Say to wisdom, 'you are my sister,' and call understanding your intimate friend" (Proverbs 7:4).

HIS COMPASSION

"And seeing the multitudes, He felt compassion for them because they were distressed and downcast like sheep without a shepherd" (Matthew 9:36-38). The only hope we have is to have a shepherd, the Shepherd. He seeks those who would worship Him in Spirit and truth (John 4:23).

Do we find ourselves self sufficient, needing no one, nor desiring to serve others? If so, we are without our leader. We will wind up as the blind do—in the ditch.

He felt compassion on a large group and healed their sick (Matthew 14:14). Compassion heals, sees the needs, and then does something about it. But too many of us "walk on the other side."

At that time, Jesus told His apostles, "They do not need to go away. You give them something to eat!" (Matthew 14:16). Had you ever noticed that? *You feed them!* Could they, the apostles, *really* have fed them? I think so. He had given them power previously to cast out demons and do miracles, but this must have seemed too large a miracle to attempt. I wonder how many times we should attempt a big project of mercy and lack the faith or will to do it! (Don't forget Satan is ever whispering in your ear, "You cannot do this!")

"And disembarking, He saw a great multitude, and He felt compassion for them because they were like sheep without a shepherd, and He began to teach them many things" (Mark 6:34). Compassion gives time, precious time, needed time, to stop and teach. To throw out the life-line to the bewildered sheep who are shepherdless.

Note that every time Jesus felt compassion, He acted on that feeling. He healed them; He fed them, He soothed their frustrated hearts, and then He taught them. Compassion, too, will make us reach out to the distressed and hurting, to feed the hungry, and to teach others. We often have to feed people before we can teach them.

THE WIDOW'S SON

Jesus saw a funeral procession passing by. The corpse was a young man, the only son of a grieving widow (Luke 7:11-17). A large crowd followed the bier. "The Lord saw her, He had compassion on her, 'Do not weep.' " He touched the bier and said, "Young man, I say to you, arise!. . .and Jesus gave him back to his mother."

Have you ever mentally pictured that scene, helping the young man up, and then giving him back to his mother's arms? What a touching scene that must have been! It stirred the crowd, and someone said, "God has visited His people." What a visitor! Compassion makes the onlooker think of the goodness of God, even today.

THE WEEPING WOMEN

"And there were following Him a great multitude of the people, and the women who were mourning and lamenting Him. But Jesus turning to them said, 'Daughters of Jerusalem, stop weeping for Me, but weep for yourselves and for your children. For behold, the days are coming when they will say, 'Blessed are the barren, and the wombs that never bore, and the breasts that never nursed" (Luke 23:28).

This passage has been a mystery to me for many years. A casual reading might leave the impression that Jesus was reprimanding those who loved Him as He was going to the cross. Why would the gentle Jesus do that? (Haven't you wished *you* could have been one who didn't run away but stood with Him, showing your love and support to the end, like Mary Magdalene did?)

Not she with traitorous kiss her Savior stung.
Not she denied Him, with unholy tongue—
But she, while apostles shrank, did dangers brave.
Last at the cross and first at the grave.

Anon.

The apostles ran in fear as was prophesied. "Then Jesus said to them, 'You will all fall away because of Me this night for it is written (Zechariah 13:7) 'I will strike down the shepherd and the sheep of the flock shall be scattered' " (Matthew 6:31).

I believe now, speaking of the weeping women, that the Lord was saying, "My death is predestined; I must die. But I know who I am and where I am going. In just a little while I will be home forever, and I know what heaven is like. But, in just a few years (about 37) you will suffer and suffer and suffer (72 AD)."

Matthew 24:21 and 22 says, "For then there will be a great tribulation such as has not occurred since the beginning of the world until now, nor ever shall. And unless those days had been cut short, no life would have been saved; but for the sake of the elect those days shall be cut short."

Jesus is saying to them, "Weep for yourselves—weep for your children that you now have and for those precious children yet to come. I'll make it. I am a strong man. I have to die for all my sheep so they can follow me, whatever the cost. I am going to prepare a place for you."

Could we have a better example of His gentleness?

And whom did He take with Him into Paradise? The least of them. A guilty thief, a repenting thief, a humbled man. Isn't that just like Jesus? What a sight that must have been! Two men with nail-scarred hands! The Shepherd and a new sheep, entering Paradise together.

Our flesh cannot grasp His love,
But yet we follow, yes, we follow.
The price He paid for our redemption;
May it not be hollow, no, not hollow.
Someday, we'll see Him face to face,
Eat from His table, partake His grace,
Never again to be tempted to fall—
But sing the story—"Heaven is worth it all."

Lea Fowler

Read or sing together:

SHALL I CRUCIFY MY SAVIOR?

Shall I crucify my Savior, When for me He bore such loss?
Shall I put to shame my Savior? Can I nail Him to the cross?

Are temptations so alluring? Do earth pleasures so enthrall
That I cannot love my Savior well enough to leave them all?

'Twas my sins that crucified Him: Shall they crucify Him yet?
Blackest day of nameless anguish, can my thankless soul forget?

O the kindly hands of Jesus, pouring blessings on all men,
Bleeding, nail-scarred hands of Jesus? Can I maim them once again?

Chorus:

Shall I crucify my Savior? Crucify my Lord again?
Once, O once I crucified Him: Shall I crucify again?
Mrs. Frank Breck

QUESTIONS FOR DISCUSSION

1. Name some results of compassion today.

2. How can we be greatest in the kingdom?

3. How does Jesus feel about the poor? How do we feel?

CHAPTER 3

THE FEEDER

The word shepherd means, "feeder." (The Lord is my feeder, He sustains my life, He provides my every need.)

"The flocks are not fed in pens or sheep-folds, but summer and winter they must depend on foraging for their sustenance."

"In the winter of 1910-1911 a terrible storm ravaged Northern Syria. Snow fell more than three feet, and it covered the ground for weeks. Hundreds of thousands of sheep and goats perished, not so much from the cold as from the fact that they could get no food." I.S.B.C.

The goats can hunt out feeding places, but sheep have to be led to their food. "May the Lord, the God of the spirits of all flesh, appoint a man over the congregation; who will go out and come in before them, and who will lead them out and bring them in that the congregation of the Lord may not be like sheep which have no shepherd" (Numbers 27:15-17).

These words were said to God by Moses when he realized his shepherding days were over. God heard his petition and provided the people with a wonderful new shepherd, Joshua.

We find Jesus giving a similar request to His followers:

> *And seeing the multitudes, He felt compassion for them, because they were distressed and downcast like sheep without a shepherd. Then He said to His disciples, "The harvest is plentiful, but the workers are few. Therefore, beseech the Lord of the harvest to send out workers into His harvest (Matthew 9:36-38).*

PROMISES OF PSALM 23

We see in this psalm how fully the needs of the sheep are supplied by the Shepherd.

1. The Lord is my Shepherd. (Men are not.)
2. My wants will be supplied. (All my needs.)
3. He leads me into green pastures. (Where I can rest.)
4. He leads me beside the still waters. (Not raging and deep waters.)
5. He restores my soul. (Forgives my sins.)
6. He keeps me on righteous paths. (His word is perfect.)
7. Even though I walk through the valley of the shadow of death. (I am never alone.)
8. I fear no evil. (God is greater than Satan.)
9. Thy rod and staff comfort me. (I am protected.)
10. A table is prepared for me in front of my enemies. (His favor is evident.)
11. He anoints my head with oil. (I am an honored guest.)
12. My cup overflows. (I will always have enough.)
13. Surely goodness and loving kindness will follow me. (I am overwhelmed by His love.)
14. I will dwell in the house of the Lord forever. (I will live with Him forever.)

THE BEDOUINS

The Bedouins still live in the Holy Land. Their tents dot the hillsides. They carry their homes to the green pastures.

We Christians are similar to them in that we, too, are pilgrims without a home. On a trip to the Holy Lands, I saw these tents, and many songs came to my mind. Such as, "This World Is Not My Home," "Here We Are But Straying Pilgrims," "Lead Me Gently Home, Father," and "I Am a Stranger Here."

You might find this interesting: On this trip I saw a Bedouin girl, leading a large flock of sheep across a busy road. I remarked to the guide that it must be dangerous for a female to be alone on deserted mountainsides. He said it was still the custom that if one of their women is harmed, the guilty man and seven of his family would be hunted down and killed. (I doubt they have to enforce this practice very often!)

HE KNOWS OUR NEEDS

How does the shepherd know one sheep from another in a large flock? They all look alike to me—but not to Him. Each sheep has its own name. And, each sheep knows its shepherd's voice and comes when it is called.

Our Shepherd, Jesus, has told us that He knows our names and even knows the number of hairs on our head! He assures us that He knows when a sparrow falls, and we should be comforted that we are worth much more than sparrows.

> *"Do not be anxious then, saying, 'What shall we eat?' or 'What shall we drink?' or "With what shall we clothe ourselves?' For all these things the Gentiles eagerly seek; for your heavenly Father knows that you need all these things" (Matthew 6:31-32).*

Do we hear, heed, follow our Shepherd? How many of *us* have had to worry about being hungry or not having a bed to sleep in at night? Or do we get side-tracked as the Gentiles did—eagerly seeking the luxuries of the world? Are we ever mindful that we are just travelers and that home is where He is? Anywhere else is a poor substitute with a bad ending.

> *Why do you spend money for what is not bread,*
> *And your wages for what does not satisfy?*
> *Listen carefully to Me, and eat what is good,*
> *And delight yourself in abundance.*
> *Incline your ear and come to Me.*
> *Listen, that you may live (Isaiah 55:2-3).*

ARE WE HUNGRY?

Read John 6:48-66. The feeder says, "Eat me. I am the bread of life." This was a difficult thought to many of His disciples. Some were offended. "As a result of this many of His disciples withdrew and were not walking with Him anymore" (John 6:66).

At a hasty reading, this teaching *is difficult.* But, it is explained in verse 63. "It is the Spirit who gives life, the flesh profits nothing, *the words that I have spoken* to you are spirit and are life."

Eat My words; fill your mind—your spirit—with everything I teach, and you will lack nothing. "The law of the Lord is perfect, restoring the soul" (Psalm 19:7). The word has lost none of its power through the ages. The Good Shepherd wants us to love His words in return for His love to us. It would please Him if we could say, as David said,

> *"And I shall delight in Thy commandments, which I love. And I shall lift up my hands to Thy commandments, which I love; and I will meditate on Thy statutes" (Psalm 119:47-48).*

CONCLUSION

No one can "learn" us or force-feed us. The feast is prepared for those who "hunger and thirst for righteousness." We, too, can gratefully say with David, *"I* shall not want." Because our Shepherd walks before us, finding the right places for us to graze.

We are often hungry and do not know
Just what it takes for us to grow.
Every need has been supplied,
We can eat to the fill, be satisfied.
With the Book closed, we are bereft.
In the midst of a feast
We can starve to death.

Lea Fowler

Read or sing together:

BREAK THOU THE BREAD OF LIFE

Break thou the bread of life, Dear Lord, to me,
As Thou didst break the loaves beside the sea;
Beyond the sacred page I seek Thee, Lord,
My spirit pants for Thee, O Living Word.

Bless Thou the truth, Dear Lord, to me—to me,
As Thou didst bless the bread of Galilee;
Then shall all bondage cease, all fetters fall;
And I shall find my peace, My All in all.

Thou art the bread of life, O Lord, to me,
The holy word the truth that saveth me;
Give me to eat and live with Thee above;
Teach me to love Thy truth, for Thou art love.

QUESTIONS FOR DISCUSSION

1. In John 6:48-63, what was Jesus teaching about Himself?

2. How can we become unashamed workers in the word?

3. What need does the Bible not supply?

CHAPTER 4

THE VOICE OF THE SHEPHERD

Many shepherds keep their flocks at night in one enclosure. When morning comes, the shepherds arrive; the gate is opened, and the shepherds separate the sheep by calling them. The sheep know their own shepherd's voice and gather around him.

> *Truly, truly, I say to you, he who does not enter by the door into the fold of the sheep, but climbs up some other way, he is a thief and a robber. But he who enters by the door is a shepherd of the sheep. To him the doorkeeper opens, and the sheep hear his voice, and he calls his own sheep by name, and leads them out. When he puts forth all his own, be goes before them, and the sheep follow him because they know his voice. And a stranger they simply will not follow, but will flee from him, because they do not know the voice of strangers (John 10:1-5).*

Isn't it a thrill to know that He not only knows when a sparrow falls—but that He knows *us* by name? Even the hairs on our head are numbered! He has our name written in His book—and even on His hands. "But Zion said, 'The Lord has forsaken me, and the Lord has forgotten me.' " "Can a woman forget her nursing child, and have no compassion on the son of her womb? Even these may forget, but I will not forget you. Behold, I have inscribed you on the palms of My hands; your walls are continually before Me" (Isaiah 49:14-16).

Jesus knows our names and claims us when we continue to hear His voice. When we quit following Him, we are in danger of being lost, in the darkness, on a lonely mountain-side.

WHY SHOULD WE HEAR THE SHEPHERD'S VOICE?

Because we must trust Him for our very existence. Because we must trust Him for our food. Because we must trust Him for our water, warmth, protection and direction. But, most of all, we must trust Him for the *safety of our souls!*

We are warned to not listen to the strangers. There have always been and will always be many "strangers." People who are teaching a different gospel—an alien doctrine.

> *I am amazed that you are so quickly deserting Him who called you by the grace of Christ, for a different gospel; which is really not another; only there are some who are disturbing you, and want to distort the gospel of Christ. But even though we, or an angel from heaven, should preach to you a gospel contrary to that which we have preached to you, let him be accursed. As we have said before, so I say again now, if any man is preaching to you a gospel contrary to that which you received, let him be accursed (Galatians 1:6-9).*

Let him be accursed. Some versions say, "anathema"—utterly cut off from God. We do not dare to add to the Word or take away from it. "It is a terrifying thing to fall into the hands of the living God" (Hebrews 10:31). "And the Scripture cannot be broken" (John 10:35).

Many deceivers are in the world, and vulnerable as we are, we are often deceived. Philosophers woo us. We can be lazy sheep who do not recognize the voice of a predator, one who will not spare the flock.

WHY DON'T WE HEAR HIS VOICE?

There are several reasons we may not hear. One is because of our own will. *We want our own way!* Daily we have to get ourselves out of the way. Do we feel we are wiser than the Shepherd?

God allows us to choose whom we will follow. This is fair. If I am lost—especially after I have taken His name—I am a victim of my own ignorance and rebellion. "But you shall speak My words to them whether they listen or not, for they are rebellious. Now you, son of man, listen to what I am speaking to you; do not be rebellious like that rebellious house. Open your mouth and eat what I am giving you" (Ezekiel 2:7-8).

Burton Coffman says, "The history of the world is a testimony to men's foolishness."

Another reason for straying away from our Shepherd is a lack of knowledge of what He has said. We are not "studying to show ourselves approved unto God." We are not "making our calling and election sure." We are not Bereans who studied the scriptures *daily* to see if what was being taught was so. *We often do not know if truth or error is being taught!*

God doesn't *make* us listen to our Shepherd's voice! If He made one person follow Him, only one, then He would be a respector of persons. Life is a result of our choices, good or bad, right or wrong. I have heard it said, "When we put anyone or anything on the throne of our heart other than Christ, we have put Him back on the cross." It is stated this way in Hebrews 6:6, ". . .since they again crucify to themselves the Son of God and put Him to shame."

Another reason for not listening to His voice is our own pride. Pride always precedes a fall. When we stop being sheep and act like goats we are butting our heads against the Rock. The Rock stands, and our "horns" are eventually broken.

BE CAREFUL HOW YOU HEAR

More understanding will be given as you grow in knowledge and expertise of the Scriptures. Remember, every time Jesus verbally responded to Satan's temptation in the wilderness, He responded with, "It is written. . ."

Do you realize that one has to *work* at listening? "Therefore, take care how you listen; for whoever has, to him shall more be given; and whoever does not have, even what he thinks he has, shall be taken away from him" (Luke 8:18). Use it or lose it.

The Word has every answer, and the Shepherd promised as He left to join the Father that He would send the Spirit to walk by our side on our journey. This Spirit, who would live in us, would be our companion, counselor, comforter, and our intercessor. We would not be left as orphans. Look up these scriptures: John 14:16-18,26; Romans 8:26-27; Acts 2:38; Acts 5:32.

HE LISTENS TO OUR VOICE

Jesus listens when we talk to Him. "When we talk to Him, He who made the world listens" (Ed Meyers). He has promised He will never leave us alone. By faith—which comes through our listening—we can become diligent disciples—learned sheep. "A disciple—one who believes His teachings, rests upon His sacrifice—imbibes His Spirit, and walks in His steps" (Farrar). (Do we study His word only to prove points or to know His will so that we may do it?)

Our finite minds cannot understand how much He loves us! He ever seeks to bring us to repentance. Are you familiar with the following verse, which could apply not only to His followers but to the world? "Or do you think lightly of the riches of His kindness, and forebearance and patience, not knowing that the kindness of God leads you to repentance?" (Romans 2:4). (Isn't it amazing and comforting to know that He was mindful of us *before* we were mindful of Him?)

The following verses have always been precious to me:

> *Oh, the depth of the riches both of the wisdom and knowledge of God! How unsearchable are His judgements and unfathomable His ways! For from Him and through Him and to Him are all things. To Him be the glory forever. Amen! (Romans 11:33,36).*

Voices call from the broader way,
Don't listen to them, whatever they say.
Their way may seem smooth and easy to trod.
But it won't lead us home,
Where we'll meet our God.
It's so important that we hear His voice,
Listen to wisdom, make Him our choice.
For their teachings are counterfeit,
They'll never ring true.
But, I'll take the genuine—
How about you?

Lea Fowler

Read or sing together:

HEAR THE SWEET VOICE

Hear the sweet voice of Jesus say, "Come unto Me,
I am the way;"
Hearken, the loving call obey; Come, for He loves
you so.

Casting your heavy burden down, Come to the cross,
the world may frown;
Yet you shall wear a glorious crown, When He makes
up His own.

Open for you the pearly gate; Loved ones for you now
watch and wait;
Terrible tho't, to cry, "too late"—"Jesus, I come
to Thee."

Chorus:

Only a step, only a step: Come, for He bled for
you and died; He's the same loving Savior yet,
Jesus, the crucified.

QUESTIONS FOR DISCUSSION

1. Where are all our answers to life?

2. Why do we sometimes not hear His voice?

3. How do we detect a stranger's voice?

CHAPTER 5

HE MAKES ME LIE DOWN

An excellent book on the 23rd Psalm is written by a former shepherd, and it is called *A Shepherd Looks At Psalm 23* by Phillip Keller. Read it if possible.

He explains why the phrase, "He makes me to lie down," is used (Psalm 23:2). Mr. Keller explains that sheep will not lie down until they are "free from all fear."

One of the fears of a flock is friction among them. Fleas and parasites also cause unrest among the flock. Another factor could be the need for them to find their own food. They must be free from hunger before they will lie down.

Their eyes must be able to see and feel the presence of the shepherd before they can be comforted and secure. They know he will supply all their needs.

FRICTION AMONG BRETHREN

We, too, have no peace when our brethren are at war. "I am for peace, but when I speak, they are for war" (Psalm 120:7). Have you ever dreaded to go to the assembly because of the discord there? Have you ever felt waves of distress among the group which has gathered? Have you ever experienced fear as a teacher taught and a listener argued? (I have, often.)

How sweet and healing are the words of David, a former shepherd.

Behold, how good and how pleasant it is
for brothers to dwell together in unity!
It is like the precious oil upon the head,

Coming down upon the beard,
Even Aaron's beard,
Coming down upon the edge of his robes.
It is like the dew of Hermon,
Coming down upon the mountains of Zion;
For there the Lord commanded the blessing—life forever (Psalm 133:1-3).

How we wish to be able to say, "I was glad when they said to me, 'Let us go to the house of the Lord' " (Psalm 122:1). (Hopefully, we have seen much more of this reaction than that of entering a disturbed assembly!)

How we can echo the thought of David when we are disturbed—"Oh, give ear, Shepherd of Israel, Thou who dost lead Joseph like a flock. . .and come to save us! Oh God, restore us, and cause Thy face to shine upon us, and we will be saved" (Psalm 80:1-3).

FLEAS AND PARASITES

There are flea and parasite problems in the church today. "It is too hot in here—it is too cold in here!" Haven't we older people sat and suffered during a sweltering worship service? Remember how we were often furnished a cardboard fan—usually with the local funeral home's picture on it? How simple it is today for women to bring a sweater, jacket or shawl for their warmth when the building is air conditioned. (I've heard lots of muttering and complaining due to women being cold.)

Another disturbance is trying to ignore crying babies. "Suffer the little children to come unto me," is a request made by Jesus—and we all have probably "suffered."

You will probably suffer far more in the mission fields than in the old established congregations. Many young couples have never been where it was expected for the children to be quiet. We could always tell without looking where a new family was sitting. But, in a short time those problems were usually handled. (Bring toys that make no noise.)

Once I saw a fine, older couple leave a service because of a screaming child whom the mother could not control. She did not know to take the child out. We begged the older couple to let us try to alter the situation, but they never returned.

In the place where we worship now, there is a lovely nursery, always serviced by women for Bible class, morning and evening worship services, and mid-week assembly. There is also a training room where parents can teach their toddlers to sit and behave on pews supplied in this room where the sermon is still seen and heard.

But, we should strive to remember the frustrations of mothers with young babies and children and *love those mothers for continuing to be faithful!* Try not to look around at them, but rather pray for them. This, too, will pass.

Crying babies may grow into annoying teen-agers. How do we endure with patience the whispering and note passing of our young people? There used to be a TV ad that said, "Parents, do you know where your children are?" Well, do we know where our teen-agers are in our worship services and what they are doing? *Have we ever grasped the reality that we alone are responsible for our kids?* Do we want other adults to have to correct our children?

Do we realize how their irreverence can keep others from communing properly? Are we aware of the scripture that says, "For he who eats and drinks, eats and drinks judgement to himself, if he does not judge the body rightly. For this reason many among you are weak and sick, and a number sleep"? (1 Corinthians 11:29-30). This is a scary thought. Many, not few, because of improper taking of the Lord's Supper are weak Christians, sick Christians, or dead Christians. Teen-agers are usually Christians themselves, and they should not only be mindful of the seriousness of Communion but should be taught by us to see that they do not disturb the worship of others.

I have heard it often said that we are known to have the worst kidney problems of all religious groups. In many congregations there is a steady stream of bored children, traipsing back and forth to the bathrooms. (I'm afraid too many adults do this, too.) How many parents are wise enough to see to it that their children are emptied out and refilled between the Bible hour and the church service? How many parents see to it that their children are then told that there will be no further trips made? (School teachers manage to get this message across.) (I have probably angered several mothers in the past paragraphs, but someone has to "bell the cat," and it is probably better if it is a great-grandmother you will never know.)

Satan will always see that things are never perfect—*especially when the saints gather!* We must learn how "not to be ignorant of his devices." Learn to close *your* eyes during Communion. Change where you are accustomed to sit to a place where you can worship in a better manner. Concentrate on blotting out the "fleas and parasites" of an assembly. Take notes on the lesson; turn to the scriptures that are read; be an active participant in the service.

FREE FROM HUNGER

We can be made to lie down in green pastures when we are fed adequately. Our Shepherd has enough "food" to feed the whole world! The One who fed the 5,000 with 5 loaves and 2 fish can supply us with enough spiritual food to get us to heaven!

But, we must be *seeking* peace and freedom from our many fears. *We* have no fear of not having enough to eat spiritually, for we are surrounded by the green pastures. The Bible is so wonderfully written that the lambs can be filled and the oldest sheep satisfied.

Jesus instructs us to cast all our anxieties to Him because He cares for us (1 Peter 5:7). He has told us to pray about everything in Philippians 4:6. *He will make us* lie down in safety, sated with a full stomach, accustomed to the gnats, strengthened to bear frictions of the flock—all because of our assurance of the Shepherd's presence!

I let such little, foolish things
Mean far too much to me.
Satan's subtle, clever schemes
Keep me from harmony.
My faith is weaker than I thought,
Would I despise my life He bought
And forget the tortured path He sought
At Calvary?

Lea Fowler

Read or sing together:

THE LORD IS MY SHEPHERD

The Lord's my Shepherd; I'll not want;
He makes me down to lie In pastures green,

He leadeth me In pastures green, He leadeth me
The quiet waters by.

My soul He doth restore again, and me to walk doth make
Within the paths of righteousness, Within the paths of righteousness,
E'en for His own name's sake.

Yea, tho' I walk in death's dark vale, Yet will I fear none ill;
For Thou art with me, and Thy rod, For Thou art with me, and Thy rod
and staff me comfort still.

My table Thou hast furnished In presence of my foes;
My head Thou dost with oil anoint, my head Thou dost with oil anoint,
And my cup overflows.

Goodness and mercy all my life Shall surely follow me;
And in God's house for evermore, And in God's house for evermore, My dwelling place shall be.

QUESTIONS FOR DISCUSSION

1. Name some things that can make Christians restless and uneasy.

2. How does Jesus help us to bear our irritations?

3. What is one of your "pet peeves" in life?

CHAPTER 6

HE RESTORES MY SOUL

He came to my desk with quivering lip
The lesson was done.
"Have you a new page for me, dear teacher?
I have spoiled this one."

I took his page, all soiled and blotted
And gave him a new one, all unspotted.
And into his tired eyes I smiled,
"Do better now, my child."

I went to the throne with trembling heart,
The year was done.
"Have you a new year for me, dear Father?
I have spoiled this one."

He took my year, all soiled and spotted
And gave me a new one, all unblotted.
And into my tired heart, He smiled,
"Do better now, my child."

Anon.

"He raised up David to be their king, concerning whom He also testified and said, 'I have found David, the son of Jesse, a man after My heart, who will do all My will. From the offspring of this man, according to promise, God has brought to Israel a Savior, Jesus' " (Acts 13:22-23).

David, an adulterer, even a murderer, was a man after God's own heart? He is to be favored in the blood line of the Savior? Why? Why?

Because David wanted, with all that was within him, to do God's will. He failed miserably but repented wholly. His soul was restored again. He bore proof of God's forgiveness to a repentant heart.

PSALM 51

In the introduction of this psalm, the NAS says, "A psalm of David, when Nathan the prophet came to him after he had gone into Bathsheba. A contrite sinner's prayer for pardon."

Let us watch in this chapter the restoration of David, the inspired writer who had said in Psalm 23:3, "He restores my soul. . ."

WASH ME THOROUGHLY

"Wash me thoroughly from my iniquity,
And cleanse me from my sin.
For I know my transgressions,
And my sin is ever before me" (Psalm 51:2-3).

Before our souls can be restored, we must realize when they are unclean in God's sight as well as ours. We must know, acknowledge, and face the consequences of our transgressions. There ought to be unrest in our hearts day and night. No peace of mind but anguish and remorse for our sin! We have to be able to admit, "I am a sinner!" (Alcoholics Anonymous teaches that there is no help until the alcoholic can say, "I am an alcoholic.")

As long as we justify our sin by any means we can think of, we cannot be healed. Sometimes, healing cannot occur until we have the courage to confess our sins to a righteous person who will pray with us and for us (James 5:16).

David asks here to be washed, to be washed thoroughly, and to feel clean again. I once heard a supposed atheist say, "How I would like to be washed all over and start again." Atheists are the most unhappy people in the world—they have no answers—just the questions. He also says in verse 7, "Wash me, and I shall be whiter than snow."

We often sing, "Lord Jesus, I long to be perfectly whole; I want Thee forever to live in my soul; break down every idol, cast out every foe. Now wash me, and I shall be whiter than snow."

MAKE ME HEAR JOY AND GLADNESS

"Make me to hear joy and gladness, let the bones which Thou hast broken rejoice" (Psalm 51:8).

It is as if David is saying to God, "I have been miserable long enough. I remember how wonderful it was when all was well with You and me. Don't look back anymore at my stupidity. Can you blot out what I have done? Can you, would you, forget how bad it was—and *help me to forget?* Because I am so sorry."

LET'S START OVER

"Create in me a clean heart, O God,
and renew a steadfast spirit within me.
Do not cast me away from Thy presence,
And do not take Thy Holy Spirit from me.
Restore to me the joy of Thy salvation,
And sustain me with a willing spirit" (Psalm 51:10-12).

Give me a clean slate. We have to repent, be forgiven, and then learn to not only forgive ourselves, but also to love ourselves again before we can wholly appreciate and enjoy the joy of His salvation. "Man or woman, we must accept and love that inner being in us before we can tolerate another person coming close enough to know us and love us" (Anon.).

I used to think the scripture said "restore the joy of *my* salvation." That would be a limited joy. But, the scripture really says, "restore the joy of *Thy* salvation." Joy is one of the Spirit's gifts. Christians should be joyous people—not giddy—but realistically joyful. The joy that comes by knowing, "God's in His heaven and all's right with the world."

"What seems to grow fairer to me as life goes by is the love and the grace and tenderness of it, not its wit and cleverness and grandeur of knowledge—grand as knowledge is—but just the laughter of children, and the friendship of friends, and the cozy talk by the fire, and the sight of flowers, and the sound of music" (Anon.).

We cannot have this measure of a good life with the basics wrong—with our relationship with God soured. We must start over with a new resolve, a forgiveness of sins through our sincere repentance, and a conscious continuing disposal of the past. As Paul said, ". . .forgetting what lies behind and reaching forward to what lies ahead, I press on toward the goal. . ." (Philippians 3:13b-14a).

RESULT OF HIS RESTORATION

"Then I will teach transgressors Thy ways, and sinners will be converted to Thee" (Psalm 51:13).

It seems like David is saying, "Now that my life is clean again, I am ready to go back to work! To do what I am created for—which is to teach transgressors and to convert sinners."

We cannot be effective workers with an unsavory, unforgiven past. Nor do we want to don the robe of the hypocrite who strives to hide his sins.

Our past should make us more understanding with others who have not yet had God's joy renewed in them. Paul taught us that we should become all things to all men so that we might win some (1 Corinthians 9:22). We should ever be mindful how easy it is to trip and fall. "He that thinketh he standeth, take heed lest he fall" (1 Corinthians 10:12).

THE REQUIRED ATONEMENT

> *"The sacrifices of God are a broken spirit; a broken and a contrite heart, O God, Thou wilt not despise" (Psalm 51:17).*

David is saying here that God is not wanting a literal sacrifice of animals, money, or things. We cannot by charity or good works buy a clear conscience. We cannot cover our sins by extra service or self-denial. *There must be a broken heart.* An humble heart of heart-felt repentance and knowledge that we cannot, of ourselves, offer sufficient retribution. God alone can read the mind, can know our sincerity—or lack of it. He knows when we are broken, naked, ashamed, and when our only hope is to reach for His hand which is reaching for ours. Reaching for us through His mercy and love.

THE RESTORATION

> *"By Thy favor do good to Zion;*
> *Build the walls of Jerusalem.*
> *Then Thou wilt delight in righteous*
> *sacrifices,*
> *In burnt offering and whole burnt offering;*
> *Then young bulls will be offered on Thine*
> *altar" (Psalm 51:18-19).*

Now David could think clearly of his position as king and his work to be done. And we, too, can find our place to serve. We can delight our God with "righteous sacrifices"! We will be running on the inside of the track again, running lawfully—with our eyes on the prize.

David is restored again, renewed to his purpose in life. He is clean, joyous, busy—complete. We can learn our lessons through his repentance and restoration.

"Restore to *me* the joy of Thy salvation."

Thy word stirs my heart,
My sins are not few.
How is my life, according to You?
Set my feet on Your path;
Clean my soul, joys renew.
Mend my broken-up heart
Which I hold out to You.
Lea Fowler

Read or sing together:

I AM SO GLAD

I am so glad that my Father in heav'n
Tells of His love in the Book He has giv'n;
Wonderful things in the Bible I see;
This is the dearest, that Jesus loves me.

Tho I forget Him and wander away,
Still He does love me wherever I stray;
Back to His dear loving arms would I flee,
When I remember that Jesus loves me.

O if there's only one song I can sing
When in His beauty I see the great King,
This shall my song in eternity be:
O what a wonder that Jesus loves me.

Chorus:

I am so glad that Jesus loves me, Jesus loves me,
Jesus loves me;
I am so glad that Jesus loves me, Jesus loves even me.

QUESTIONS FOR DISCUSSION

1. Name some joys of His salvation.

2. What kind of a heart does God love?

3. How do we cultivate a good conscience?

CHAPTER 7

THE COMFORTING ROD

"Even tho I walk through the valley of the shadow of death, I fear no evil, for Thou art with me. Thy rod and Thy staff, they comfort me" (Psalm 23:4).

DEFINITION OF THE ROD

"Figurative of Divine guidance and care." I.S.B.S.

Matthew Henry comments on these words with the following: "Tho I am under the arrest of death, have received the sentence of death within myself, and have all reason in the world to look upon myself as a dying man, I am easy."

THE SHADOW OF DEATH

We all begin to die when we are born. There is only one way out of this life, this world, and it is death. (Unless the Lord comes in our lifetime.) Why do we fear it so? The shadow is there daily. But, death is not an enemy if we are prepared. Death has no sting if eternal life with God beckons. Rather, it is a release from pain and suffering.

> *Since then the children share in flesh and blood, He Himself likewise also partook of the same, that through death He might render powerless him who had the power of death, that is, the devil; and might deliver those who through fear of death were subject to slavery all their lives (Hebrews 2:14-15).*

Jesus conquered death when He arose from the grave never to die again. He fulfilled the prophecy of Genesis 3:15 that Satan's head would be bruised though only His heel would be bruised. "And I will put enmity between you and the woman, and between your seed and her seed; He shall bruise you on the head and you shall bruise him on the heel." The strong man was bound and can no longer plunder our houses, for our house is built on the foundation of Christ. "Or how can anyone enter the strong man's house and carry off his property, unless he first binds the strong man? And then he will plunder his house" (Matthew 12:29).

I WILL FEAR NO EVIL

God even monitors our fears and many afflictions.

> *Many are the afflictions of the righteous but the Lord delivers him out of them all. He keeps all his bones; not one of them is broken. Evil shall slay the wicked, and those who hate the righteous will be condemned (Psalm 34:19-21).*

It is only the unsaved who should fear pain, afflictions, and death. There lives are tormented because of their actions and their unanswered problems. They live in the shadow of death without the Shepherd and are surrounded by darkness. There is no light, no path for their feet. And that is not what God wants for any man.

But, as for Israel, He says, "All the day long I have stretched out to a disobedient and obstinate people" (Romans 10:21). They have not heeded the "good news." They are without comfort though the answer to their fears has already been offered. *We are to be the comfort carriers.* Are *we* about our Father's business?

FOR THOU ART WITH ME

Oh, that we sheep could only realize that He is *always* with us. "The eyes of the Lord are toward the righteous and His ears are open to their cry" (Psalm 34:15). The Shepherd is ever watching the flock that He knows by name. He is seeing to their needs, feeding and watering them, bedding them down safely. He never sleeps.

He is mindful of the hungry predators who are looking for the tasty lambs. He is aware of how quickly we can be in serious trouble that we cannot handle, and our bleating gets His attention. The Bible is full of accounts of wicked people hating the righteous. Ahab killed innocent Naboth. Many prophets were slain by their own people. Saul tried for years to kill David.

In Psalm 34:16 and 17, we read, "The face of the Lord is against evil doers, to cut off the memory of them from the earth. The righteous cry and the Lord hears and delivers them out of all their troubles." But, someone may say, "Naboth wasn't delivered, and the prophets were killed." The Lord doesn't promise that the righteous won't meet death violently, though few do in this time of little perecution. But, He does promise that He is there. He hears them. *And He will have the last say!*

We are taught not to fear those who have the power to kill our bodies. They do not have the power to kill our soul. God was with Stephen when he died, and His reflection lightened the very countenance of Stephen who prayed for his enemies as he died.

THE ROD COMFORTS ME

When Jesus was about to leave the apostles, He promised them He would not leave them as orphans. He would send the Comforter, the Holy Spirit. This Helper would be in them and with them to the end. "And I will ask the Father, and He will give you another Helper, that He may be with you forever; that is the Spirit of truth, whom the world cannot receive, because it does not behold Him or know Him, but you know Him because He abides with you and will be in you. I will not leave you as orphans. . ." (John 14:16-18).

Today we have the same promise. He has gone to prepare a mansion for us and has given us the indwelling of the Holy Spirit. "And we are witnesses of these things; and so is the Holy Spirit whom God has given to those who obey Him" (Acts 5:32). As we pray, and nobody knows how to pray as one should, this Helper hears our groanings and puts them into an acceptable wordage to the Father who searches the hearts and knows the mind of the Spirit (Romans 8:26-27). So, we are comforted. This is part of the rod's use—"The Divine guidance and care."

Have you ever in an emergency prayed in such a way that a bystander would know your hysteria but would not understand what you were asking for? If you haven't yet, you probably will pray that way. Often it is just saying, "No! No! No!" Yet, your petition is understood and brought to God's throne and explained by the Spirit. *And what a comfort that is!*

THY ROD COMFORTS ME

A shepherd always carried a rod, a staff, a stick, for protection, for help to walk and if needed, as protection for the flock. We often think of a hook on the end of the staff. This hook could be used to rescue a sheep from a precarious position on the mountains.

As the flock followed the shepherd, the staff could often be seen by the sheep. When we keep our spiritual eyes on our Shepherd, we, too, are greatly comforted by seeing that He knows the way and has the means of delivering us, too, from precarious positions. His love is from everlasting to everlasting.

Are you feeling like I am? Are your eyes moistened with unshed tears? Do you feel secure, warm and safe? Are you assured of His presence, His power, and His love? Are you tasting the peace and joy that passes understanding—peace and joy that the world never tastes?

We should no longer be afraid in the valley of the shadow of death. We know He is with us, and we are comforted by His rod and His staff. There is no need for any fear. "Trust in the arm that is strong to defend us."

I used to be afraid of death,
To lose my life, to lose my breath.
But now I know I'm not alone
For I am His, His very own.
The home unseen will be so sweet;
I just can't wait until my feet
Are walking on the golden road
And I lay down this heavy load.

Lea Fowler

Read or sing together:

O MASTER, LET ME WALK WITH THEE

O Master, let me walk with Thee
In lowly paths of service free;
Tell me Thy secret, help me hear
The strain of toil, the fret of care.

Help me the slow of heart to move
By some clear, winning word of love;

Teach me the wayward feet to stay,
And guide them in the homeward way.

In hope that sends a shining ray
Far down the future's broad'ning way,
In peace that only Thou canst give,
With Thee, O Master, let me live.

QUESTIONS FOR DISCUSSION

1. What are some of our fears?

2. Give a Bible example of God's deliverances.

3. Give an example of God's deliverance for you in an emergency.

CHAPTER 8

THE NINETY AND NINE

What more can the Godhead do than They have done and are still doing to show Their followers how involved They are in the world and in the church? Our finite minds are limited in grasping the omniscient (all knowing), omnipotent (all powerful), and omnipresent (ever present) existence and work of the Father, the Son, and the Spirit.

Hopefully, each of us is growing spiritually. We are leaving our childhood and growing towards adulthood in Him. Paul reminded the Corinthian babes in 1 Corinthians 3:1-3:

> *And I, brethren, could not speak to you as to spiritual men, but as to men of flesh, as to babes in Christ. I gave you milk to drink, not solid food; for you were not yet able to receive it. Indeed even now you are not yet able, for you are still fleshly. For since there is jealousy and strife among you, are you not fleshly, and are you not walking like mere men?*

THE LOST SHEEP PARABLE

This parable is told to show the care and protection of Jesus for the flock, the church, the disciples, the followers. He knows when one of His is out in the dark—alone, defenseless, scared and hurting. And, He does something about it.

> *See that you do not despise one of these little ones, for I say to you, that their angels in heaven continually behold*

the face of My Father who is in heaven. (For the Son of Man has come to save that which was lost.) What do you think? If any man has a hundred sheep, and one of them has gone astray, does he not leave the ninety-nine on the mountains and go and search for the one that is straying? And if it turns out that he finds it, truly I say to you, he rejoices over it more than over the ninety-nine which have not gone astray. Thus it is not the will of your Father who is in heaven that one of these little ones perish (Matthew 18:10-14).

This parable is told twice. The account in Matthew emphasizes the care of the Son of Man for one of the "little ones." A caution is given to be mindful of those in the flock who are often neglected and deemed unimportant. Human nature tends to seek out and impress the favored few. We are often influenced by power and riches while God is mindful of weakness and poverty of spirit. "Blessed are the poor in spirit, for theirs is the kingdom of heaven" (Matthew 5:3).

James speaks to both the poor and rich in James 1:9. "But let the brother of humble circumstances glory in his high position. . ." (What high position? His position of equality in the church. Poor and rich commune together, give together as they are prospered, sing and pray together as they grow together. God makes somebodies out of nobodies.)

". . .and let the rich man glory in his humiliation, because like flowering grass, he will pass away." (What humiliation does the rich Christian bear? He isn't loved for his wealth but for his life. He isn't or shouldn't be given special attention or respect because of his bank account, or clothes, or job, or education. God makes nobodies out of somebodies.)

Now all the tax gatherers and the sinners were coming near Him to listen to Him. And both the Pharisees and the Scribes began to grumble, "This man receives sinners and eats with them." And He told them this parable, saying, "What man among you, if he has a hundred sheep and has lost one of them, does not leave the ninety-nine in the open pasture, and go after the one which is lost, until he finds it? And when he has found it, he lays it on his shoulders, rejoicing. And when he comes home, he calls together his friends and his neighbors, saying to them, "Rejoice with me, for I have found my sheep which was lost!" I tell you that in the same way, there will be more joy in heaven over one sinner who repents, than over ninety-nine righteous persons who need no repentance (Luke 15:1-7).

In Luke's account of the parable, the emphasis is on the mercy of Jesus upon the tax gatherers and sinners. We are reminded of Jesus giving an invitation to the good and the bad for the wedding feast of the Son. In Matthew 22:9 and 10 we read, "Go therefore to the main highways, and as many as you find there, invite to the wedding feast. And those slaves went out into the streets, and gathered together all they found, both evil and good; and the wedding hall was filled with dinner guests."

The joy of the shepherd is mentioned here. The joy in finding one lost sheep—"and when he has found it, he lays it on his shoulders, rejoicing. And when he comes home, he calls his friends and neighbors to rejoice with him." Can you imagine the joy of the sheep that was found? The one who was lost without hope on a dark mountain? Oh, the security of hearing the voice of the shepherd and then the comfort of being carried home around his neck—or in his bosom!

ANGELS REJOICE

The end of the parable is so important. "I tell you that in the same way, there will be more joy in heaven over one sinner who repents, than over ninety-nine righteous persons who need no repentance" (Luke 15:10).

COMPARISON OF THE PARABLES

"Christ spoke this parable twice, evidently for a different purpose on each occasion. In this instance (Matthew 18:10-14), it stands for the infinite love and solicitude the Lord has for the very least of His children; but in Luke's account of it (Luke 15:1-7), it appears to have been spoken as an argument against the Pharisees who would go to a lot of trouble for a lost animal but had no regard for a lost man. The parables are the same, but they are spoken with significant variations."

"In the scripture, goats are used to represent sinners and sheep represent Christians. The lost sheep, therefore, represents a child of God who has become a backslider, who is separated from the fold, and from the Shepherd" (Coffman).

A HUNDRED SHEEP

A man would be thought well-off who owned a hundred sheep in those days. "The seeking after the lost sheep shows the eager desire to find it, it does not show that he thinks more of the one sheep than he did of the ninety-nine. The ninety-nine were left and the concern about them was suspended until the lost was found" (Boles).

THE PHARISEES

Many Pharisees thought themselves better and more righteous than anyone else. They often lacked compassion. Do we ever *dare* compare ourselves to them? Do *we* really seek others to be saved? Are we mindful of brethren who are straying from the fold? Are we interested in the babes, the lambs, or the poor or the weak of the flock? Do we seek only the righteous as the Pharisees did? Do we show partiality?

"But if you show partiality, you are committing sin and are convicted by the law as transgressors" (James 2:9).

"But once you allow any insidious distinctions to creep in, you are sinning. You stand condemned by the law" (Phillips).

We don't get to pick the sheep that we want in the flock. The Shepherd does. It's His flock!

Do we heed, hear, follow our Lord? Do we ever find ourselves needing sustenance, necessities? Or instead, do we get side-tracked as the "Gentiles" did—eagerly seeking the things we don't need? Things of the world, the amassing of riches that will be left behind. *Travelers should not pick up more than they can carry.* "Why do you spend money for what is not bread, and your wages for what does not satisfy? Listen carefully to Me, and eat what is good, and delight yourself in abundance. Incline your ear and come to Me. Listen, that you may live" (Isaiah 55:2-3).

THE END OF THE PARABLE

The flock was together again. The lost sheep was found. The friends and neighbors returned home with thankful hearts. The party was over. The shepherd could rest now. The ninety and nine could rest, too. The shepherd realized he had saved a sheep from death, for he knew how vulnerable it was.

"It is absolutely defenseless, having no weapon of any kind, no gift of speed in flight, no cunning, no means of deception, its very cries being only a signal for the enemy to close in for the kill. Let every backslider behold here his helplessness apart from Christ" (Coffman).

THE SHEPHERD'S CRY

Don't take your eyes off Me,
The wilderness is death, you see.
I have a fold where safety lies,
It's filled with food and all supplies
That are necessary for you to rise
And come and live with Me.
Lea Fowler

Read or sing together:

THE NINETY AND NINE

There were ninety and nine that safely lay
In the shelter of the fold,
But one was out on the hills away,
Far off from the gates of gold;
Away on the mountains wild and bare,
Away from the tender Shepherd's care.
(Repeat last line.)

Lord, Thou hast here Thy ninety and nine
Are they not enough for Thee?
But the Shepherd made answer This of mine
Has wandered away from me,
And altho the road be rough and steep,
I go to the desert to find my sheep.
(Repeat last line.)

But none of the ransomed every knew
How deep were the waters crossed
Nor how dark was the night that the Lord passed thru
Ere He found His sheep that was lost.
Far out in the desert He heard its cry.
'Twas sick and helpless and ready to die,
(Repeat last line.)

But all thru the mountains, thunder riv'n
And up from the rocky steep,
There arose a glad cry to the gate of Heav'n,
Rejoice I have found My sheep.
And, the angels echoed around the throne,
Rejoice for the Lord brings back His own,
(Repeat last line.)

QUESTIONS FOR DISCUSSION

1. Why do sheep stray?

2. What are some signs that a sheep is straying?

3. What can help bring us back to the fold?

CHAPTER 9

THE SHEPHERDS ON EARTH

"Obey your leaders, and submit to them; for they keep watch over your souls, as those who will give an account. Let them do this with joy and not with grief, for this would be unprofitable for you" (Hebrews 13:17).

It is God's plan for the church to have earthly shepherds over the flock. Shepherds should be chosen by the Holy Spirit and carry out the will of the Chief Shepherd. What a blessing to have consecrated God-chosen men, who set the example for us to follow! What burdens they bear that the flock is unaware of! The sleepless nights, the unsolved problems, the burden of sheep who stray, and even sometimes, their own yearnings to be free from such grave responsibilities.

THEY WATCH FOR OUR SOULS

Elders are to watch out for our souls. They must ever seek to keep us safely in the sheep-fold, the church. They are to be aware of the dangerous pits ahead and the predators who lie in wait to destroy the flock.

The good sheep will listen to their voices, but the goats will seek other leaders or go their own way. Strange as it may sound, I heard an antagonistic woman say one day, "I'm just not going to do what the elders say and then they are going to have to answer to God for my decision!" On another occasion, when the elders had announced there would be something new at the following service, a member remarked,

"Well, whatever it is, I'm against it!" (The member did not know that the new addition was a microphone at the Lord's Table!)

When our elders seek us out to help us, we should be aware of their good intentions and honor them for their concern for our welfare. It is human nature to be on the defensive at these times, but we must keep our hearts open to their efforts for the unity of the body and our own salvation.

PETER WAS AN ELDER

> *"Therefore, I exhort the elders among you, as your fellow-elder and witness of the sufferings of Christ and partaker also of the glory that is to be revealed, shepherd the flock of God among you, not under compulsion, but voluntarily, according to the will of God; and not for sordid gain, but with eagerness; nor yet as lording it over those allotted to your charge, but proving to be examples to the flock. And when the Chief Shepherd appears, you will receive the unfading crown of glory. You younger men, likewise, be subject to your elders; and all of you, clothe yourselves with humility toward one another, for God is opposed to the proud, but gives grace to the humble" (1 Peter 5:1-5).*

Peter is saying to elders, "Eagerly give up your time, your own will, always remembering you have a charge to keep. You have a flock to defend, to nourish, to love, and to hold in the place of safety until He returns. Remember you are not a lord, but always a shepherd, a bishop, a presbyter—one who is a follower himself of the Chief Shepherd, carrying out His will for His flock." (One has to learn to follow before he can lead others.)

There is a crown awaiting a faithful elder, but I think the greatest delight to him will be seeing the eternal safety of the flock he led.

THE HOLY SPIRIT APPOINTMENT

> *"Be on guard for yourselves and for all the flock among which the Holy Spirit has made you overseers, to shepherd the church of God which He purchased with His own blood; I know that after My departure savage wolves will come in among you, not sparing the flock; and from among*

your own selves men will arise, speaking perverse things, to draw away the disciples after them" (Acts 20:28-30).

We do not have to understand the way the Holy Spirit makes men overseers. We do know the inspired word gives the qualifications of elders. Take the time and read what the Holy Spirit has said in 1 Timothy 3:1-7 and Titus 1:5-9.

In reading these qualifications, does the church see Christian men who have these qualities? Do these men see these qualities in themselves? Do they desire to be servants in this wonderful, difficult, time-consuming labor? Are they leading and working already? Are they apt Bible students? Are their own families under the control of these men? Is hospitality a part of their lives? Are they kind? Are they easily angered and hard to entreat? Would you seek them out for counselling a difficult, personal problem?

In choosing elders, we must let the Holy Spirit guide us and not be swayed by our own emotions, prejudices, or likes and dislikes. We often forget that the church is not a democracy where we vote on the man we like—but the church is a kingdom, with Christ as our head. The men that are selected to serve as elders must meet the qualifications that God and the Holy Spirit have set forth—not our own!

God knows what the mind of the Spirit is. "And He who searches the hearts knows what the mind of the Spirit is, because He intercedes for the saints according to the will of God" (Romans 8:27).

A NEED FOR ELDERS

In Titus 1:10-11, we read, "For there are many rebellious men, empty talkers; and deceivers, especially those of the circumcision, who must be silenced because they are upsetting whole families, teaching things they should not teach, for the sake of sordid gain."

It is God's plan for His shepherds to protect the flock from the many who misteach because they don't understand the Scriptures. These men need to be silenced by the elders because they are destroying a whole flock due to their own ignorance.

DESPISED AUTHORITY

Any authority will always be unpopular with many! The private hates the sergeant; the sergeant despises the general, and the general has little respect for the President. God is very explicit about those who hate authority.

> *"Then the Lord knows how to rescue the godly from temptation, and to keep the unrighteous under punishment for the day of judgement, and especially those who indulge the flesh in its corrupt desires and despise authority. Daring, self-willed, they do not tremble when they revile angelic majesties, whereas angels, who are greater in might and power do not bring a reviling judgement against them before the Lord" (2 Peter 2:9-11).*

These people described were not sheep, were not meek, were not followers. They were goats. They knew better, but they "butt" their wills against God's authority. Listen to Titus 3:10-11: "Reject a factious man after a first and second warning, knowing that such a man is perverted, and is sinning, being self condemned."

Guy N. Woods says in regard to 2 Peter 2:9-11, "Despite the fact that they knew the penalty for their conduct, they defied the Lord; and arrogant, audacious, and proud, they blasphemed dignities—all authorities without fear. These words indicate the extreme coarseness, insolence, and hardness of heart characteristic to these false teachers."

YEAKLEY'S REPORT

Yeakley, a gatherer of the church's statistics, says that it usually takes 20-25 years for local churches to grow qualified men to serve as elders. It is interesting to note that Titus was told to appoint "elders in every city in Crete." We learn that the churches in Crete were approximately 34 years old at this time. Cretians were at Pentecost—33 AD—and Titus was supposedly written in 67 AD, 34 years after the church was established on Pentecost.

HOW DO WE FEEL ABOUT ELDERS?

Do we love them? Do we respect them? Do we try to keep ourselves in line with God, each other, and the elders? Do we realize that they are watching out for our very souls? Maybe I have just been blessed, but I have never been a part of a body of Christ where I didn't love my elders.

Mothers, are we teaching our lambs to love and follow the shepherds? In fact, do we teach them to respect *all* who are in authority—school, government, and church? *Our children will pick up on our attitudes on authority!*

ACCUSATIONS OF ELDERS

"Let the elders who rule well be considered worthy of double honor, especially those who work hard at preaching and teaching. For the Scripture says, 'You shall not muzzle the ox while he is threshing,' and 'The laborer is worthy of his wages.' Do not receive an accusation against an elder except on the basis of two or three witnesses" (1 Timothy 5:17-19). Do we find ourselves guilty for looking for flaws in the ones who are leading? Are we quick to accuse and condemn? Are we too judgmental? May we have the courage, if we find ourselves wanting in this matter of submission to leadership, to review our own trespasses and return to the fold.

Phillip Morrison has said, "Many years ago an older friend told me that if a congregation had access to all the information its elders had, the congregation would make exactly the same decision as the elders made. My own observations through the years lead me to the same conclusion. Sometimes people want to test that theory by sharing with the congregation everything known to the elders. But that isn't desirable or advisable. People who have sought eldership counsel about intimate, personal problems are entitled to the strictest confidentiality. And some matters not confidential in nature may be too complex and involved to be mastered by a large group. The church is not a democracy; it is a kingdom whose King has charged elders with the responsibility for congregational leadership."

An elder is a man with a heavy load,
Trudging down an uncharted road,
Sheep at his feet, lambs at his heels.
He leads by faith, not as he feels.
He knows the Shepherd will not let him down,
But He'll give at the end a God-blessed crown.

Lea Fowler

Read or sing together:

SAVIOR, LIKE A SHEPHERD LEAD US

Savior, like a shepherd lead us:
Much we need Thy tend'rest care;
In Thy pleasant pastures feed us,
For our use Thy fold prepare;
Blessed Jesus, Blessed Jesus,
Thou hast bought us, Thine we are;
Blessed Jesus, Blessed Jesus,
Thou has bought us, Thine we are.

Early let us seek Thy favor,
Early let us do Thy will;
Blessed Lord and only Savior,
With Thy love our bosoms fill:
Blessed Jesus, Blessed Jesus,
Thou hast loved us, love us still;
Blessed Jesus, Blessed Jesus,
Thou hast loved us, love us still.

QUESTIONS FOR DISCUSSION

1. How many elders should be serving in a congregation?

2. Name some God-given qualifications for elders.

3. Do you encourage your elders by word and deed?

CHAPTER 10

THE HIRELING

"He who is a hireling and not a shepherd, who is not the owner of the sheep, beholds the wolf coming, and leaves the sheep, and flees, and the wolf snatches them, and scatters them. He flees because he is a hireling and is not concerned about the sheep" (John 10:12-13).

A good shepherd is "the feeder" of the sheep. He willingly provides for their every need. A hireling is a laborer who works only for his wages. He has no personal feeling of responsibility for the welfare of the flock.

THE SELFISH HIRELING

"He is a hireling who would not work were it not for the money he receives. He only cares for his own selfish end. He will lead the flock away from hope with false doctrines when popularity lends its influence in that direction" (Boles).

Job mentions a hireling in Job 7:2, "As a slave who pants for the shade, and as a hired man who eagerly waits for his wage." This man is a clock watcher, one who makes a great pretense of hard labor when the boss is around. He is one who feels contempt for his job and for his employer.

A WORTHLESS SHEPHERD

A description of the worthless shepherd is given in Zechariah 11:17: "Woe to the worthless shepherd who leaves the flock! A sword will be on his arm and on his right eye. His arm will be totally withered, and his right eye will be blind."

The King James says instead of the worthless shepherd—the idol shepherd. The thought here is that this man is like an idol who cannot see or hear. He willingly receives praise and honor, undeserved, but is not able to do any kindness. He runs from the flock when they need him the most! He is interested only in saving his own skin—let the flock he is paid to serve be destroyed while he survives!

HIS PUNISHMENT

Matthew Henry remarks on this scripture this way: "His arm and right eye will become useless. In time he won't know how to save himself. No longer will he be able to see or be strong enough to deliver the flock even if he wanted to. Those that have gifts which qualify them to do good, if they do not do good with them shall be deprived of them; those that should have been workmen, but were slothful and would do nothing, will justly have their arm dried up; and those that should have been watchmen but were sleepy and would never look about them, will justly have their eye blinded."

DAVID, THE SHEPHERD

David was an example of the good shepherd. He killed a lion and a bear who would have harmed the flock. He protected the sheep at the risk of his own life. But that experience gave him the faith to face Goliath with only 5 stones and a proven sling-shot.

Goliath sneered as he saw the young man approaching. "And the Philistine (Goliath) said to David, 'Am I a dog that you come to me with stones?' And the Philistine cursed David by his gods" (1 Samuel 17:43).

David had already reassured his own people of his approaching victory. "The Lord who delivered me from the paw of the lion and from the paw of the bear, He will deliver me from the hand of the Philistine" (1 Samuel 17:37). (David didn't have to worry about his arm withering or his eye becoming blind.) "Use it or lose it," is ever a faithful maxim.

LESSONS TO BE LEARNED

We could or may die in our own battles against Satan. Many Christians have. But, we must remember our past victories and deliverances and be encouraged in times of unexpected peril. We are not to fear him who can only kill the body, for death is not the end of the story. Matthew 10:28 says, "And do not fear those who kill the body, but are unable to kill the soul; but rather fear Him who is able to destroy both soul and body in hell."

A scripture came to mind as I read this one above. "You will not be afraid of the terror by night, or of the arrow that flies by day; of the pestilence that stalks in darkness, or of the destruction that lays waste at noon. A thousand may fall at your side, and ten thousand at your right hand; but it will not approach you. You will only look on with your eyes and see the recompense of the wicked" (Psalm 91:5-8).

David's only hope was God. No one could hear him cry for help on the mountain-side with his flock. He was alone with his beloved sheep, and he risked his life for their protection. Who was it that said, "A coward may die a thousand deaths, but a brave man only one"?

GOD GIVES US COURAGE

Paul reminds us that God does not give us this feeling of fear. "For God has not given us a spirit of timidity, but of power and love and discipline!" (2 Timothy 1:7). This was spoken by the old apostle Paul to his son in the gospel, Timothy. No doubt Paul's heart ached for the young man and the troubles that were yet to be for Timothy. (I remember as a missionary's wife how often *my* heart ached for the young preachers' wives who came to New England. These were women who had left their parents and friends to walk in an unfamiliar land, trying not to look back to home. My spiritual side said to myself, "Stay, it is worth it all!" But, my physical side often wanted to say, "Go home, this is too hard!" Thank God, I never said it.)

THE EPHESUS WILD BEASTS

Paul fought with the "wild beasts" as he called them. "If from human motives I fought with wild beasts at Ephesus, what does it profit me? If the dead are not raised, let us eat and drink, for, tomorrow we die" (1 Corinthians 15:32).

In checking two commentaries on this verse, Coffman thinks it is likely that Paul had a literal fight with some beast at Ephesus. (We know that many Christians were thrown to the lions long ago.) Matthew Henry says it this way: "I take it, therefore, that this fighting with beasts is a figurative expression, that the beasts intended were men of a fierce disposition."

Brethren can be used by the Lord to build up the church or can be used by Satan to try to destroy the church. We must ever be aware that when the saints meet, Satan still comes, too, just as he did in Job's time (Job 1:6; 2:1).

We must remember that the church will survive because it belongs to the One who gave His life for it. This Good Shepherd watches day and night over His flock.

He knows where the hirelings are.

"Son of Man, prophecy against the shepherds of Israel. Prophecy and say to those shepherds, 'Thus says the Lord God, "Woe, shepherds of Israel who have been feeding themselves! Should not the shepherds feed the flock? You eat the fat and clothe yourselves with the wool, you slaughter the fat sheep without feeding the flock. Those who are sickly you have not strengthened, the diseased you have not healed, the broken you have not bound up, the scattered you have not brought back, nor have you sought for the lost; but with force and with severity you have dominated them and they were scattered for lack of a shepherd, and they became food for every beast of the field and were scattered. . .Thus says the Lord God, behold, I am against the shepherds, and I shall demand My sheep from them and make them cease from feeding sheep. So the shepherd will not feed themselves anymore, but I shall deliver My flock from their mouth, that they might not be food for them. For thus says the Lord God, behold, I Myself will search for My sheep and seek them out as a shepherd cares for his herd in the day when he is among his scattered sheep, so I will care for My sheep and will deliver them from all the places from which they were scattered on a cloudy and gloomy day" (Ezekiel 34:2-5,10-12).

(It would be good to read this entire chapter.)

CONCLUSION

Yes, we know that there are hirelings among elders. Some love the office instead of the service. Some love to dominate to such an extent that an entire congregation limps along under an iron rule. Other elders are too meek and cannot defend the truth or themselves.

Pray for your elders. Pray for their leadership and courage. And pray for their continued growth. Remember that God sees all and in His time, He will right the wrongs.

May our Shepherd watch o'er us
And the Spirit choose
The men who will follow His lead.
And help us to stay on the difficult path,
To follow in word and in deed.

Lea Fowler

Read or sing together:

A CHARGE TO KEEP I HAVE

A charge to keep I have, A God to glorify,
A never-dying soul to save, And fit it for the sky.

To serve the present age, My calling to fulfill;
O may it all my powers engage To do my Master's will!

Arm me with jealous care, As in Thy sight to live,
And O, Thy servant, Lord, prepare, A strict account to give!

Help me to watch and pray, And on Thyself rely,
Assured, if I my trust betray, I shall forever die. Amen.

QUESTIONS FOR DISCUSSION

1. Name some characteristics of a hireling.

2. Compare hirelings and Pharisees.

3. How can we be prepared to detect error in teaching?

CHAPTER 11

THE DEATH OF THE SHEPHERD

So, the Shepherd died according to The Plan, and the Scriptures were fulfilled concerning His death. We sheep who were each going our way caused His death. "All of us like sheep have gone astray, each of us has turned to his own way. But the Lord has caused the iniquity of us all to fall on Him" (Isaiah 53:6).

It took me many years to understand the necessity for the death of Christ. I knew many facts, but I couldn't connect them. Here they are:

1. All who can sin have sinned. "When they sin against Thee (for there is no man who does not sin)" (1 Kings 8:46). "For all have sinned and fall short of the glory of God" (Romans 3:23).

2. Death is the sentence for all sinners. "The soul that sins shall die" (Ezekiel 18:4). "The wages of sin is death" (Romans 6:23).

3. God allowed Someone to die in our place. He accepted a substitution, expiation, satisfaction, or propitiation in our place. "And He Himself is the propitiation for our sins; and not for ours only, but also for those of the whole world" (1 John 2:2).

4. Christ's motive for dying in our stead was His love for us. "In this is love, not that we love God, but that He loved us and sent His Son to be the propitiation for our sins" (1 John 4:10). Also John 3:16.

All these facts kaleidoscoped in my mind when I comprehended the following scriptures:

Blessed be the God and Father of our Lord Jesus Christ, who has blessed us with every spiritual blessing in the heavenly places in Christ, just as He chose us in Him before the foundation of the world, that we should be holy and blameless before Him.

In love He predestined us to adoption as sons through Jesus Christ to Himself, according to the kind intention of His will,

to the praise of the glory of His grace, which He freely bestowed on us in the Beloved.

In Him we have redemption through His blood, the forgiveness of our trespasses, according to the riches of His grace,

which He lavished upon us. In all wisdom and insight

He made known to us the mystery of His will, according to His kind intention which He purposed in Him

with a view to an administration suitable to the fullness of the times, that is, the summing up of all things in Christ,

things in the heavens and things upon the earth, in Him

also we have obtained an inheritance, having been predestined according to His purpose who works all things after the counsel of His will (Ephesians 1:3-11) (Phillips).

In other words, putting it all together—before the world was created, the Godhead had planned that after sin was in the world, there would be a way back to God through Christ. The first man sinned and all men after him sinned, too. God's justice demanded death. But, God's mercy allowed the death of Christ, His blood, to cleanse us, and we could become holy and blameless through Him who died in our stead. Love devised The Plan—love beyond our finite understanding, "according to the kind intention of His will."

He died for us while we were yet still in our sins, without hope, strangers. "Remember that you were at that time separate from Christ, excluded from the commonwealth of Israel, and strangers to the covenants of promise, having no hope and without God in the world. But now in Christ Jesus you who formerly were far off have been brought near by the blood of Christ" (Ephesians 2:12-13).

THE GOOD SHEPHERD

The Good Shepherd laid down His life for His sheep. He came into the world, a "man of sorrows," knowing His destiny.

> *I am the Good Shepherd; and I know My own, and My own know Me, even as the Father knows Me and I know*

the Father; and I lay down My life for the sheep. . .For this reason the Father loves Me, because I lay down My life that I may take it again (John 10:14-15,17).

When the time came to die, the man in Christ didn't want to die anymore than we would have wanted to die. Daily He had seen the many Roman crosses with their tortured men dying or dead. He knew that it would be an excruciatingly slow death. And yet, He also knew that no one would take Him against His will, but rather He would be an offering of love for us, His sheep, and for those who would seek Him in all ages.

THE FULLNESS OF TIME

The fullness of time occurred when crucifixion was the manner of punishment. "But when the fullness of the time came, God sent forth His Son, born of a woman, born under the Law" (Galatians 4:4).

The cross was to be a symbol of not only suffering and shame, but also a lifting up of the Savior to be seen by those who would receive Him. "And I, if I be lifted up from the earth, will draw all men to Myself. But He was saying this to indicate the kind of death by which He was to die" (John 12:32-33).

Isaiah, the Messianic prophet, had prophesied that Christ would be crushed, oppressed, afflicted, a guilt offering poured out to death and would be numbered with the transgressors (Isaiah 53).

Today there is nothing administered by law that could compare to the pain of the cross. Death sentences are now quick—such as, the gas chamber, the electric chair, or the firing squad. These are merciful deaths compared to the death that our Shepherd suffered!

Why would anyone want to kill the Good Shepherd who carried the lambs in His bosom and looked out for the nursing ewes? "Like a shepherd He will tend His flock, in His arm He will gather the lambs, and carry them in His bosom; He will gently lead the nursing ewes" (Isaiah 40:11). Why would the innocent be killed for a guilty sinner? Because, *He died in our stead*—He died for us and paid the price. We were the ones who should have hung on that cross, suffered the agonizing death—of all people, it should have been us! But, it was this Messiah, this Savior who made this decision for us, and paid that expensive price with His precious blood!

What a travesty of justice! The peasants were killing their King! The created were torturing their Creator. An angry mob was killing an unresisting Shepherd. "For consider Him who has endured such hostility by sinners against Himself, so that you may not grow weary and lose heart" (Hebrews 12:3). "In humiliation His judgement was taken away" (Acts 8:33).

WHAT HELD HIM ON THE CROSS?

I have often wondered and will never know in this life, "Did it make it easier or harder for Him to know He could stop it all if He chose to?" Surely the angels coming to Him in the garden when He prayed for another way out helped enormously to strengthen Him.

While the crowd jeered and challenged Him to save Himself and they would believe, while the women wept in deep sympathy and pain, while He gave His mother to the apostle of love, was it easier or harder to have the power to stop it all and save Himself? He *could* have called 10,000 angels!

What held Him there? Many things. His love for the sheep and the world. The joy that was set before Him gave Him the power to continue to endure the pain. The joy of going home. He *knew* how wonderful heaven was! He *knew* the fellowship of the Father and the Spirit. *He knew who He was and where He was going.*

He also had the power of foreknowledge of the many saints who would later die torturous deaths and could not spare themselves as He could. He had forewarned His apostles of their future persecutions and deaths. (History says that all of the apostles but John were violently killed.) Why was John spared? He, too, had fled when Jesus was seized. It had been prophesied that when the Shepherd was struck, the sheep would flee (Zechariah 13:7). But John came back. He was at the cross, and there is no mention of any other apostle being there. He stood close enough for Jesus to speak personally to him and entrust His own mother to him.

Of course, I can't know why John was spared a violent death. But, I wonder if the answer is not found in Matthew 16:25: "For whoever wishes to save his life shall lose it; but whoever loses his life for My sake shall find it." John was willing to risk his life, if necessary to be crucified himself, and perhaps it was this commitment to Christ that allowed him to be exiled and not murdered.

THE FINAL THOUGHT

If we who are in Him, are the flock of God, what comfort it should be *that we are so loved!* Jesus did pay it all! The account is settled. The Plan has been carried out. Now it is up to us.

Believers should not perish.

Be with our finite minds
As we study from the word.
May we grasp the truths revealed
And the story which we've heard
Of the Shepherd and His sheep
And His love for all mankind.
May we follow to the end
With our hearts and with our minds.

Lea Fowler

Read or sing together:

ON A HILL FAR AWAY

On a hill far away stood an old rugged cross,
The emblem of suffering and shame;
and I love that old cross where the dearest and best
For a world of lost sinners was slain.

O that old rugged cross, so despised by the world,
Has a wondrous attraction for me;
For the dear Lamb of God left His glory above,
To bear it to dark Calvary.

In that old rugged cross, stained with blood so divine,
A wondrous beauty I see;
For 'twas on that old cross Jesus suffered and died,
To pardon and sanctify me.

To the old rugged cross I will ever be true,
Its shame and reproach gladly bear,
Then He'll call me some day to my home far away,
Where His glory forever I'll share.

Chorus:

So I'll cherish the old rugged cross,
Till my trophies at last I lay down;
I will cling to the old rugged cross,
And exchange it some day for a crown.

QUESTIONS FOR DISCUSSION

1. Why did Christ have to die?

2. When was the plan for the atonement made?

3. Explain the timing of His death.

CHAPTER 12

THE SLAIN LAMB

"And I saw a Lamb standing as if slain. . .for Thou wast slain and didst purchase for God with Thy blood men from every tribe and tongue and people and nation. . ." (Revelation 5:6,9).

It was prophesied that Christ's character would be like a lamb and that His death would be accepted as the perfect sacrifice for the sins of the world. "He was oppressed and He was afflicted, yet He did not open His mouth; like a lamb that is led to slaughter, and like a sheep that is silent before the shearers so He did not open His mouth" (Isaiah 53:7).

This is such a touching scene! It would have been expected for Him to resist, to wrestle, to defend Himself against torture and slaughter. But when they came to arrest Him, He asked them why they came with swords and clubs. "Am I a robber?" He asked. He reminded them that He had often sat and taught in the temple unarmed.

No, you don't need a sword or a club to capture and kill sheep. They don't know how to resist. God knows we, too, don't know the dangers that daily surround us, nor do we realize how often we are delivered from evil and harm!

THE SIN OFFERING

A lamb was killed under the old law to substitute, satisfy, or atone for the sins of the one who offered it. Surely, many offered this animal by faith, not understanding why it took a death, blood, to cover sin. "And without the shedding of blood there is no forgiveness" (Hebrews 9:22).

We now live under the perfect law—the whole truth has been revealed. We can see how much God hates sin and that all sin must be punished, for the "wages of sin is death." God is not mocked or fooled by men's devices, but He will bring all hidden things into the light. Jesus, by His sacrificial death, provided a way for God's mercy and a way to be saved from His wrath.

The blood of the Lamb not only can cover the sins of those under the new law, but also it flows back to cover the sacrifices made under the old law. Romans 3:24-25 says, "Being justified as a gift by His grace through the redemption which is in Christ Jesus; whom God displayed publicly as a propitiation in His blood through faith. This was to demonstrate His righteousness, because in the forbearance of God He passed over the sins previously committed."

"For God sent Christ Jesus to take the punishment for our sins and to end all God's anger against us. He used Christ's blood and our faith as the means from saving us from His wrath. In this way He was being entirely fair, even though He did not punish those who sinned in former times. For He was looking forward to the time when Christ would come and take away those sins. And now in these days He can receive sinners in this same way, because Jesus took away their sins." L.B.

Someone taught it this way, and it often comes to my mind. When people sacrificed the animals under the old law, Jesus gave them a post-dated check. When He died, the price for the sins under the old law was paid, and the sins were forgiven. The blood flowed back to Adam and flows forward to the last person who will be saved by it.

When Jesus asked the Father for another way to die—not the cross—there was no other way. "For this reason came I into the world." He was the perfect lamb without spot or blemish, and *He offered Himself.* He did not have to be subdued or forced, but He walked, carrying His own heavy cross on His wounded back. As the old song says, "Hallelujah, what a Savior!"

MARRIAGE OF THE LAMB

Revelation 19:7-9 says, "Let us rejoice and be glad and give the glory to Him, for the marriage of the Lamb has come and His bride has made herself ready. And it was given to her to clothe herself in fine linen, bright and clean; for the fine linen is the righteous acts of the saints. And He said to me, 'Write, Blessed are those who are invited to the marriage supper of the Lamb.' And He said to me, 'These are true words of God.' "

The Lamb lives again! Though He was slain, yet He arose and someday will return to receive His bride, the church. There is so much symbolism in the Bible. Jesus is called the Lamb, the Rock, the foundation of the church, the King, the Bridegroom and the Shepherd. Each of these words describe His character, His work, and His nature.

We who are being saved should be preparing ourselves for this marriage. We must be bright and clean, without spot or blemish or wrinkle. (We do beautify ourselves in His eyes as we turn from sin and turn to righteousness.)

THE LAMB'S BOOK

When this world has ended, the trumpet has sounded; then, the sheep will be gathered in to the sheep-fold. There will be no need for light there, for the lamp is the Lamb. "And the city has no need of the sun or of the moon to shine upon it, for the glory of God has illumined it, and its lamp is the Lamb" (Revelation 21:23).

Who are these sheep who will be written in the Lamb's book of life? Only those who have been redeemed by His blood. Redeemed means to be bought back. We are to be the sheep who no longer turn to our own way. We are to realize how expensive the price to redeem us was! We are to realize afresh the cost for our salvation each Lord's Day as we commune. "Knowing that you were not redeemed with perishable things like silver and gold from your futile way from life inherited from your forefathers, but with precious blood as of a lamb unblemished and spotless, the blood of Christ" (1 Peter 1:18-19).

IS OUR NAME IN THE BOOK?

We are cautioned to "make our calling and election sure." Satan would like to deceive us and keep us from examining our conversion or present lifestyle. "Therefore, brethren, be all the more diligent to make certain about his calling and choosing you. . ." (2 Peter 1:10).

There are many callings today with their own ideas for the soul. It is easier to hear their voice than to investigate. Too often we are like baby birds, in the nest with our mouths wide open to swallow whatever is put in them. If we hunger for truth and righteousness, *we shall be filled!* That is a promise from God.

We are warned about false prophets and man-made doctrines. "You therefore, beloved, knowing this beforehand, be on your guard lest being carried away by the error of unprincipled men, you will fall away from your own steadfastness. But grow in the grace and knowledge of our Savior Jesus Christ" (2 Peter 3:17-18).

BENEDICTION

"They shall hunger no more, neither thirst anymore, neither shall the sun beat down on them, nor any heat; for the Lamb in the center of the throne shall be their Shepherd, and shall guide them to the springs of the water of life; and God shall wipe every tear from their eyes" (Revelation 7:16-17).

They didn't really have to force Him
To the cross, He'd gladly go,
There was no other way to save us,
From the sins we've done below.
There was no other way to meet Him
In the everlasting land,
No other way to be forgiven
Than in the washing of the Lamb.
Lea Fowler

Read or sing together:

O SACRED HEAD

O sacred head, now wounded, With grief and shame weighed down.
Now scornfully surrounded With thorns Thine only crown;
How art Thou pale with anguish, With sore abuse and scorn;
How dost that visage languish, Which once was bright as morn!

What language shall I borrow To thank Thee, dearest Friend,
For this Thy dying sorrow, Thy pity without end?

O make me Thine forever; And, should I fainting be,
Lord, let me never, never, Outlive my love to Thee.

QUESTIONS FOR DISCUSSION

1. Why are you glad God looks on us as lambs?

2. How can we be sure our names are in His book?

3. What do you look forward to the most in heaven?

CHAPTER 13

THE DIVISION OF THE FLOCK

When the church, the flock, was begun in 33 AD, there was only one Shepherd and only one flock. "There is one body and one Spirit, just as also you were called in one hope of your calling; one Lord, one faith, one baptism—one God and Father of all who is over all and through all and in all" (Ephesians 4:4-7). (One "body" signifies the one church—Ephesians 1:22-23.)

It was the plan before the foundation of the world made by the Godhead that the flock "should be holy and blameless before Him" (Ephesians 1:4b). But, from the beginning, there were many other teachers who taught a different doctrine. Even the early elders of the church were warned that among themselves there would be perverse teachings given to draw away members after themselves (Acts 20:30).

A DAY FIXED

For at least 2,000 years there has been a day fixed for the end of the world.

> *Therefore having overlooked the times of ignorance, God is now declaring to men that all everywhere should repent, because He has fixed a day in which He will judge the world in righteousness through a Man whom He has appointed having furnished proof to all men by raising Him from the dead (Acts 17:30-31).*

People in all ages have scoffed at this teaching. Many have jeered at this thought because every day has been like the day before. 2 Peter 3:3-4 says, "Know this first of all, that in the last days mockers will come with their mocking, following after their own lusts, and saying, 'Where is the promise of His coming? For ever since the fathers fell asleep, all continues just as it was from the beginning of creation."

God reminds them that this world goes on as usual because the Word that spoke the world into existence also keeps the world functioning. And in this same chapter He reminds us that all is temporary, and the Great Day is coming.

> *But the day of the Lord will come like a thief in which the heavens will pass away with a roar and the elements will be destroyed with intense heat, and the earth and its works will be burned up. Since all these things are to be destroyed in this way, what sort of people ought you to be, in holy conduct and godliness, looking for and hastening the coming of the day of God, on account of which the heavens will be destroyed by burning, and the elements will melt with intense heat! But according to His promise we are looking for new heavens and a new earth, in which righteousness dwells. Therefore, beloved, since you look for these things, be diligent to be found of Him in peace, spotless and blameless (2 Peter 3:10-14).*

Ever since the church was established and to this day, there are the faithful and the unfaithful. By our works all shall be known. Jesus taught that the kingdom would have the good and the bad in it, the sheep and the goats.

> *Again, the kingdom of heaven is like a dragnet cast into the sea, and gathering fish of every kind; and when it was filled, they drew it up on the beach; and they sat down, and gathered the good fish into containers but the bad they threw away. So it will be at the end of the age; The angels shall come forth, and take out the wicked from among the righteous, and will cast them into the furnace of fire; there shall be weeping and gnashing of teeth (Matthew 13:47-50).*

PROTECTION OF THE FLOCK

"The Lord is my Shepherd, I shall not want" is recorded by David. These same promises were given by Moses at the beginning of the Law to God's people. And they were renewed under the New Law to God's people. We are taught in Matthew 6:25-34 that we will have our necessities in life provided. *We, too, shall not want!* However, that is on the condition that we will put "the kingdom and His righteousness" first in our lives (Matthew 6:33).

THE CATTLE AND THE CATTLE

Ezekiel points out that not all sheep were the good sheep and that judgement would be made among the flock.

> *Therefore, thus says the Lord God to them, "Behold, I even I, will judge between the fat sheep and the lean sheep. Because you push with side and with shoulder, and thrust at all the weak with your horns, until you have scattered them abroad, therefore, I will deliver My flock, and they will no longer be a prey; and I will judge between one sheep and another. Then I will set over them one shepherd, My servant David, and he will feed them; he will feed them himself and be their shepherd" (Ezekiel 34:20-23).*

Continue reading through verse 31 for a list of promised blessings that God gives to His flock. He closes with, "As for you, My sheep, the sheep of My pasture, you are men, and I am your God."

Matthew Henry comments on the above scripture. "It has been observed concerning sheep that if one of the flock be sick and faint the rest will secure it as well as they can, and shelter it from the scorching heat of the sun—but these, on the contrary, (the goats) were most injurious to the diseased."

He also observes that the reference "could be to the scribes and Pharisees who devoured widows' houses, took away the key of knowledge. . .oppressed the consciences of men with the traditions of the elders, and were continually vexatious and injurious to the poor of the flock of God."

THE HYPOCRITES

The hypocrite (who is thought a sheep) is like the Pharisee who looks out only for himself. Ezekiel 34:18-19 says, "Is it too slight a thing that you should feed in the good pasture, that you must tread down with your feet the rest of your pasture? Or that you drink of the clear waters, that you must foul the rest with your feet? And as for My flock, they must eat what you tread down with your feet, and they must drink what you foul with your feet!"

THE FAT AND THE STRONG

"I will seek the lost, bring back the scattered, bind up the broken, and strengthen the sick, but the fat and the strong I will destroy; I will feed them with judgement" (Ezekiel 34:16). The supposedly "fat and strong" are those who will face God's judgement. They will be condemned for not looking after the least of the flock. The least had to eat the trampled grass and drink the muddied water.

THE SHEEP ON THE RIGHT

But, one day, any day, we will see this judgement spoken by Ezekiel. Jesus also taught clearly that the Shepherd will separate the sheep from the goats.

> *But when the Son of Man comes in His glory, and all the angels with Him, then He will sit on His glorious throne. And all the nations will be gathered before Him; and He will separate them from one another, as the shepherd separates the sheep from the goats; and He will put the sheep on His right, and the goats on the left. Then the King will say to those on His right, "Come, you who are blessed of my Father, inherit the kingdom prepared for you from the foundation of the world" (Matthew 25:31-34).*

The sheep will be on the right. There will be no mistakes in the selections. The books have been kept, and no errors are possible.

THE JUDGEMENT STANDARD

The good sheep are full of the nature of the Spirit of God that we see listed in Galatians 5:22-23. They will be full of love, joy, peace, patience, kindness, goodness, faithfulness, gentleness, and self-control. These are attributes given by the Spirit as sheep grow in grace and knowledge. Who would fear sheep (people) with these qualities?

Many believers think that we will be judged *only* by our faith. But the sheep on the right will be judged by the faith that works. James reminds us that faith without works is a dead faith (James 2:26). The Scriptures teach us that there are many kinds of faith—vain, strong, weak, and dead.

THE LEAST OF THEM

The good sheep look after the injured sheep—"the least of them." Who are the injured? The hungry, the thirsty, the strangers, the naked, the sick, and the poor. Do the least of them seek us out—or more importantly, *do we seek them?* Do we reach for those that Jesus would seek or do we search only for our acceptable peers? When will we realize that we are now treating the Shepherd in the way we treat the least of *them?* Does this trouble your heart or your conscience? *It does mine.* Does it trouble us enough for us to determine to change? Or are we only seeking those who need no physician? Time will tell.

THE GOATS ON THE LEFT

Here again there will be no mistakes made nor any need for any regrouping. Goats represent the willful who seek only their own way. They are not doers of the word nor do they listen to the Shepherd's voice. They do not serve and are guilty of partiality. They look out for "number 1." Instead of the fruits of the Spirit, the fruits of the flesh are evident in them:

If we are not wise and we hastily read the list of the fruits of the flesh (Galatians 5:19-21), we will quickly disclaim any likeness to this list. We say to ourselves, "We are not guilty of idolatry, sorcery, drunkenness, adultery, or carousing!" But, are we guilty of enmities, strife, jealousy, anger, disputes, dissensions, envyings, or factions? (As the old joke goes—"You quit preaching and went to meddling!") Surely, we have all at one time or another been guilty of most of that list.

THE JUDGEMENT GIVEN

. . ."Then He will answer them, saying, 'Truly I say to you, to the extent that you did not do it to one of the least of these, you did not do it to Me.' And these will go away in to eternal punishment, but the righteous into eternal life' " (Matthew 25:45-46). "You *did not do* to the least of them, so you did not do to Me," the Savior says. "If you had been more mindful of the unfortunate, their stories might have ended differently. *They might have become sheep.*"

Jesus fed people first and then taught them. His friends were the poor and the rich. The lepers, the blind, the lame, as well as Nicodemus and Joseph of Arimathea—wealthy men. Love was in His eyes—people felt free to touch Him and love Him back! He was there in the emergencies! He wept with the mourners, as He weeps with us today. He looked at the heart and not at a man's wrappings.

Mary and Martha were probably women of means, but they were two of His closest friends. He ate with Zaccheus, a wealthy tax collector, who probably had been very dishonest. Jesus chided the rich host who spurned a sinful woman. He lifted up the woman caught in adultery and delivered her from a "religious" mob with stones in their hands. He taught the Samaritan woman who had been married five times and was living with a man and turned her into a personal worker. And so on, and so on.

TWO DIFFERENT ENDINGS

To the sheep on the right He said, "Come, you who are blessed of my Father, inherit the kingdom prepared for you from the foundation of the world" (Matthew 25:34).

Jesus had told us in John 14:2-3. . ."for I go to prepare a place for you. And if I go and prepare a place for you, I will come again, and receive you to Myself; that where I am there you may be also." Those on the right will be *truly* "blessed of the Father." A battle has been won; the faith has been kept, and the victor's crown awaits the veteran's head.

But the goats on the left will hear a far different summation. "Depart from Me, accursed ones, into the eternal fire which has been prepared for the devil and his angels" (Matthew 25:41).

The spirit of man never dies. That is probably what God meant when He said, "Let Us make man in Our image" (Genesis 1:26). Hell was not in God's plan for mankind. "Behold, I have found only this, that God made men upright, but they have sought out many devices" (Ecclesiastes 7:29).

Nothing unclean will enter heaven. "And nothing unclean and no one who practices abomination and lying, shall ever come into it (heaven), but only those whose names are written in the Lamb's book of life" (Revelation 21:27).

OUR YARD STICK

The sheep on the right and the left said to Him, "When did I see YOU with such needs?" And the answer was the same to each group. "Whatever you did—or did not do—*it was to Me!*" What are we using to judge ourselves? Are we measuring ourselves by what others do or don't do? Are we mindful of the example of those in the flock who are generous and impartial? Do we realize that heaven will be full of people we might have classed as "the least of them"? Will any of "them" rejoice at seeing *us* there? Will we have been helpful in their salvation? And, will we be happy to be "one" with them now? Do we get to pick out the sheep we like to be there or does the Shepherd do all the selecting? Do we hastily brand a sheep a goat when he really is a sheep?

We would do well to search our hearts and actions now. Do you remember the song that says:

"I am satisfied with Jesus
He has done so much for me.
But the question comes to me
When I think of Calvary—
Is my Master satisfied with me?"

Surely we do not want to hear the words, "To the extent that you did not do it to one of the least of these, you did not do it to Me."

The book is over; the writing is done.
Our race is ending; the battle's won.
Life is short though of many days—
Not always simple, sometimes a maze.
But what really matters, when truth I see,
How was the gospel according to me?

Lea Fowler

Read or sing together:

THERE'S A GREAT DAY COMING

There's a great day coming, a great day coming,
There's a great day coming by and by,
When the saints and the sinners shall be parted,
Right and left, Are you ready for that day to come?

There's a sad day coming, a sad day coming,
There's a sad day coming by and by,
When the sinner shall hear his doom,
"Depart, I know ye not," Are you ready for that day to come?

Chorus:

Are you ready, are you ready?
Are you ready for the judgement day?
Are you ready, are you ready?
Are you ready for the judgement day?

QUESTIONS FOR DISCUSSION

1. When do we become part of the flock?

2. How can others see if we are good sheep?

3. What goat-like qualities do I have to work on?

Epilogue

How does the Shepherd feel about His old sheep, especially those who were faithful? "Now the God of peace, who brought up from the dead the Great Shepherd of the sheep through the blood of the eternal covenant, even Jesus our Lord, equip you in every good thing to do His will, working in us that which is pleasing in His sight, through Jesus Christ to whom be the glory forever and ever. Amen" (Hebrews 13:20-21).

When we older people look back, we find He has *never left us unequipped.* He has always richly provided for our needs. We have never been alone or deserted. We are thankful that He never gave up on us but ever drew us back to Him. "For you were continually straying like sheep, but now you have returned to the Shepherd and Guardian of your souls" (1 Peter 2:25).

I will close this book with a verse that has brought to me great peace of mind. It was penned by the beloved prophet, Isaiah, who foretold so much of the nature and life of the coming Messiah, Jesus.

> *"You who have been borne by Me from birth*
> *And have been carried from the womb;*
> *Even to your old age, I shall be the same,*
> *And even to your graying years I shall bear you!*
> *I have done it, and I shall carry you;*
> *And I shall bear you, and I shall deliver*
> *you" (Isaiah 46:4).*

So, we close this book with praise and thanksgiving to the Shepherd who purchased the flock with His own blood. "So we Thy people and the sheep of Thy pasture will give thanks to Thee forever; to all generations we will tell of Thy praise" (Psalm 79:13).

I just want to be a sheep!